How To Write Your Personal or Family History

(If you don't do it, who will?)

Katie Funk Wiebe

Good Books

Intercourse, PA 17534
800/762-7171
www.GoodBooks.com

Design by Cliff Snyder

Library of Congress Cataloging-in-Publication Data
Wiebe, Katie Funk.
  How to write your personal or family history : if you don't do it, who will? /
Katie Funk Wiebe.
      p. cm.
  ISBN 978-1-56148-665-6 (pbk. : alk. paper) 1. Autobiography--Authorship--
Handbooks, manuals, etc. 2. Genealogy--Authorship--Handbooks, manuals,
etc. 3. Authorship--Handbooks, manuals, etc. I. Title.
  CT25.W453 2009
  929'.1072--dc22   2009017184

Table of Contents

PREFACE

Writing this book was a labor of love, a passion. My interest in encouraging people to write their personal or family histories began in 1978 when the head of the social work department at the college where I was teaching asked me to teach an enrichment course in writing to older adults. I was having trouble keeping my English composition students inspired. How could I inspire people three times their age who had been out of school for 40 or more years? What approach would work with this group?

As I began researching the possibilities of topics to write about, I realized the greatest riches of this group of somewhat subdued, yet still-with-it, people were their own life experiences. For six weeks I invited, cajoled, and encouraged my class of about 18 grey-haired men and women to write about what life had handed them. Their enthusiasm about having a coach to guide them, at a time when memoir-writing was just beginning, inspired me to do more.

Out of this short teaching experience came my book *Good Times with Old Times: How to Write Your Memoirs*, which remained in print for several decades.

After I retired from college teaching, I took time to research my own family story with greater energy. I traveled to the former USSR, even to Siberia, to find relatives who had disappeared into the Russian landscape with few remaining contacts with my family. I read voraciously everything I could get my hands on about how my ancestors had lived in another culture, as well as in Canada and the United States. Out of this research came several more of my writings: *The Storekeeper's Daughter,* sections in *Border Crossing,* and several self-published books about the lives of close relatives. I wrote my own autobiography, *You Never Gave Me a Name: One Mennonite Woman's Story.*

When the memoir-writing instructor at the East Wichita Shepherd's Center retired for health reasons, I stepped in. This is an inter-faith organization designed to enrich the lives of post-retirement men and women by offering a variety of courses and activities.

How to Write Your Personal or Family History is the result of my three years of teaching and handouts, answering questions, clarifying problems, and enjoying these writers who are engaged in an important life task of people my age—life review. I have included writing tips, as well as examples of writings, some by me, others by class members, and also an occasional assignment.

The great fear of new writers is the blank page. What to write? The writing of a personal or family history is not a weekend project, but one that will take months and possibly years. The process of researching, discovering, and synthesizing may well be the greatest joy and accomplishment of your life.

—*Katie Funk Wiebe*

You Have a Story Waiting to be Told

"What's new? What's going on in your life?" your friend asks.

"Not much," you say. Your date book shows only ordinary activities, such as picking up dry cleaning, phoning George regarding the board meeting, or going with Jeanie to the PTA meeting. If your house had burned down, you'd won the lottery, or endured a major plumbing breakdown, you'd have something to say. But beyond this daily routine, your mind goes blank.

Yet you've been living 24 hours every day, making decisions, objecting to certain ideas, endorsing others, and interacting with family and coworkers. In effect, just living. If you took time to reflect, you'd find lots of meaningful stuff going on.

Personal or autobiographical writing, in any of its many forms, asks you to think not only about actions (a trip to the dentist), but also feelings, attitudes, and motives, and to put them into words. It invites you to select a few of all your experiences and to give them shape and order. A reader is not interested in a trip to the dentist unless that dentist had a heart attack and died in the middle of the drilling. A reader is interested in why you voted a certain way at the board meeting against majority opinion, or why you are switching from business to truck gardening – or maybe giving up on both. Readers are interested in how you handled change or conflict.

A writer for a television drama, or a novelist, has the luxury to decide plot development beforehand. She can give the main character houses and cars by the dozen, if she wishes. She can choose his enemies and handicaps. If she doesn't like one ending, she can change it, or even kill off the protagonist as well as any supporting characters. A writer of personal history can't do that. Your life is what it is, but it is every bit as worthwhile and unique as that of a college president or Mount Everest climber.

The purpose of personal writing is to entertain, of course, but also to inform family and friends about your life, to inspire by example, and especially, to offer yourself as an example of the process of living. Writers of family histories, autobiographies, and memoirs are concerned with shaping, making sense of the past from the standpoint of a present that is different. They want readers to understand what it means to experience successes and flops, affirmations and misunderstandings, and much more, from the standpoint of someone with a wider perspective.

When I was young, I believed that my Russian-German immigrant past had no connection with who I was or would become. I hadn't hid my past from my children, but I hadn't shared it, either. I unwittingly maintained the image that I had been reared in a vacuum and was responsible for my own development. My parents spoke English with difficulty. Their syntax always had a German flavor and their pronunciation gave away their recent immigrant status immediately. Some of their customs dated back to the Middle Ages, I was sure. Their growing-up stories, I thought, had no relevance to who I was becoming.

I was like many people who want to kick away the ladder by which they arrived at the present. They rush away from the past, wanting nothing to do with it. I wanted to disconnect myself from the bedbugs, *banyas,* and revolution experiences of my parents in Russia, as well as their immigrant struggles in the strange new land of Canada. Only my present counted.

How wrong I was.

Though I wanted to discard my past, some people worship theirs. They keep leafing through old albums and memories, and never get on with the business of living. They tell one another, "It was so good in the old days when we ate fresh-baked bread every week, children played in empty sandlots, and we sat on the front verandah each evening and watched neighbors stroll past." They forget the back-breaking work of chopping wood for the stove, with its insatiable need for fuel, the lack of water to bathe sweaty children who had been playing in the dirt all day, and the absence of air-conditioning in 100-degree weather. Autobiographical writing isn't about enshrining the past.

Others drag the past into the present like a heavy trunk, burdened by past experiences. They nurse age-old grudges against parents, siblings, teachers, and church leaders. They are angry with institutions, previous employers, governments, and anyone in authority. Any mention of their past raises their hackles.

Writing about the past, retracing our steps, gives us a better understanding of it. We see it through new eyes and can make sense of the jumble of experiences. We can free ourselves of it and decide how to act in the present.

A Few Beginning Tips

Memoir writing is not newswriting using the first person. If you had been involved in a house burglary, readers would expect news articles written by different people to carry basically the same information. Autobiographical writing is different in that it gives your view of your experience. Your siblings' or another person's view of the same event might be quite different, but that's all right. Experience and viewpoint change our perceptions, as does our place in the family lineup of siblings. As I wrote once:

> My experience of communal showering is probably quite different from that of a group of 14-year-olds, accustomed to showering together in school gymnasium showers. At one retreat center, all the women showered

in one large room with a dozen or more shower heads. I gulped, removed my clothes in the dressing area, and edged slowly into the area with the shower heads, wishing the tiny washcloth I held carefully over strategic areas were a super-sized beach towel. I furtively checked out other aging bodies. Buttocks and bosoms abounded in all sizes and shapes, looking like bread dough that had ballooned and fallen in on itself. I hurriedly showered and left. Enough of this, I muttered to no one in particular. Only two more mornings to do this.

"I don't have anything to write about," I hear often. You haven't had any earth-shattering experiences. You never flew to the moon or invented a new zucchini recipe that won you glowing comments from family and friends. That's not the issue. You lived 24 hours each day, made decisions, unconsciously looked for role models, rejected certain values, and adopted others. You loved, you hated, you endorsed, you objected. Your life is unique and worthwhile. You have a story to tell. It just needs to be sorted and refined.

Sorting through life used to be done behind the plough, while nursing a child, ironing linens, shelling peas, or collecting eggs. A hurried non-reflective life makes it necessary to deliberately take time to reflect in a more structured or disciplined way just like workers with sedentary jobs now have to set aside time for exercise. Writing your personal story gives you the opportunity to reflect upon your life. It is a tool to sort through personal values, faith, and commitments.

Remember, you can't write without revealing who you are. Good writing is an exercise in self-revelation. The more personal, the more universal, I've often told classes. The exercise of writing pushes you into the exercise of being. Without sharing your inner life, you share a corpse, one workshop leader explained.

Find the truth about yourself, face it, and share it with the reader. Be willing to wear your heart on your sleeve. Readers don't know want to know how many trips you took to Alaska or Timbuktu, but what happened when life hit you with a brickbat. Readers want to know when you ran with the bulls all alone before a hostile audience. You don't need to brag, but don't hesitate to mention your achievements or even the times you just slogged along. Even slogging can make meaningful reading.

To write a personal or family history can be a daunting task. Let's sum up how this book might guide you. You don't even need to ask your doctor for an opinion on the matter.

1. Everyone has a story to tell, not just the person who won a gold medal in the Olympics. If you don't write it, who will?

2. Retrieving our stories brings meaning to life by discovering the patterns of our lives. They are a way of inspiring others to dream and dream big. Many people who have forged ahead in new areas were inspired by other models who dared to risk. "Here is someone very much like me who made something beautiful out of life," they think.

3. Writing your story helps you make peace with the past and free yourself of it. The past has a way of bludgeoning us into submission. It helps others by sharing how you dealt with issues of concern.

4. It helps you get a better sense of the life cycle and to accept it with hope. When we reflect upon and reassess life achievements and losses, we end up with better balance and contentment.

5. Your personal or family story is a way to pass on family history, folklore, values, and wisdom. It preserves a written account of the past for the sake of others. Each generation has to make its own commitments, its own promises to God and one another, but it helps if a new generation carries images of the way another generation dreamed and made promises to themselves and humanity. Your story is a way to connect with future generations.

Literary critic Alfred Kazin told a group of English teachers that language is the salvation of the immigrant child, who must reorder existence by means from within. The immigrant has only language by which to pass on important values and truths. The past is gone as well as household furnishings and other artifacts.

Kazin was an immigrant. He said, "One writes to make a home for oneself on paper — to find a place, a ledge." I understood then why my father and other immigrants were always telling stories about the "old country." At 85, he was still telling them, writing them in little bits of letters, still trying to make a whole out of the pieces of his life, and then offering them to me. "Now you work with it, Katie," he told me.

Language is also our salvation to bring order out of the confusion of modern-day life, to put together the puzzle of life. Immigrant children and today's older adults both move in a bewildering world. Everything is different and perplexing and no longer fits into old categories. I hesitate to dive into the world of text messaging, phone cameras, and BlackBerrys. I tell my son, when he introduces me to something new electronically, "Haven't I done enough?"

In this new world, I am like my immigrant parents, who brought with them to Canada few tangible artifacts, but carried within themselves a value system, memories, and hope, which can only be expressed with words. In our quickly changing society, where we're not sure what new electronic gadget will be heralded today as the best thing since sliced bread, or when we will encounter a great new medical discovery, we are all immigrants of another kind. Change is rushing at us on all fronts — technological, economic, political, social, and theological. We move about, change professions, change allegiances. Storytelling is a way of going back along the trail to learn where to make turns in the journey forward.

Young people tell me they want to write. "Write about what you know best — yourself," I say. Their faces fall. "I haven't had any experiences," they reply. "I haven't been to New York or Hollywood." As if life only happens in those two places.

I tell them, "You have lived 20, 30, or more years and have experienced nothing? What happened to the 24 hours of each day God gave you? Did you let them slip by without logging any for future reference? Go back to your past, retrieve it, and shake loose the essence of your life. Let the past live again as you learn from it and make it part of the future." That's my advice for writers at any age.

The writing of your memoirs may never stop inflation, a strike, a riot, or even a war, but it will help your readers, young and old, to understand the gift of their heritage, and to feel the ground becoming firmer under their feet. Storytelling is the place where social and personal history meet. Reading about patterns of faith, courage, and self-reliance in the face of obstacles inspires new beginnings. A knowledge of the past will give understanding of how change affects all of us and how to face an uncertain future.

So start with passion. Tell yourself: "I have to do this. This is my job. If I don't write it, who will?"

PUTTING TOGETHER THE PUZZLE OF LIFE

Writing your personal or family story is much like putting together a jigsaw puzzle. You've bought a puzzle or found it on a closet shelf. You first find a place to work where you can leave the unfinished project undisturbed. You post a warning sign: DO NOT DISTURB. Maybe you add a skull and crossbones. You're serious about this.

When I do a jigsaw puzzle, I usually work at the edges first, keeping my eyes on the picture on the box cover. Corner pieces are great finds. Sometimes I'm sure there's a missing piece, but by the time I get to the end, I've found it. Sometimes a piece is missing forever. It got caught in the vacuum cleaner or the dog ate it. Or I blame it on the manufacturer.

Eventually I have to fill in huge patches of clear blue sky or acres of green grass, maybe dense, dark undergrowth. That's the tough part. But I keep going, and finally, I find the last piece. I shout "hurrah," and rush to call the family.

The finished picture is not the real thing, but an approximation of some reality, but to show the finished product to others brightens my day. It was a big job, but I did it. Likewise, I also enjoy writing family stories and showing them to my children and siblings.

Writing your personal or family story entails much the same process. Behind you lies a jumbled mess of experiences, good and bad, as well as emotions, insights, losses, gains, and periods of stagnation and growth. You can't go to a store to find a ready-made picture of your life. You must decide how the pieces will fit together.

So what is a first step? Choose the type of picture you want to put together about your life. Ask yourself: "What will I write?" Your choice will be determined by the type of material you find and how much. But here are some categories:

Genealogy: This is the study of a family's lineage, tracing it from a distant ancestor through the various family branches. This data, which consists mainly of names and dates of birth and marriage, and information about the deaths of relatives and their children, is put on a chart. This book will not delve seriously into genealogy.

Family History: This entails documenting the details of the lives and times of yourself and/or family members, and collecting reminiscences, old letters, photos, newspaper clippings, diaries, journals, and other documents – anything related to your family and giving your findings shape. You can write this as the saga of a family or emphasize individual members. The focus is on the family as a unit and the factors that affected the family over the years.

Autobiography: The story of your own life

Biography: The story of someone else's life.

If genealogy is the bones, or skeleton, of your past, then autobiography/biography and family history are the more creative and descriptive components. They are an account of your life or someone else's, often in chronological order, a popular way to write a life story. The point of view is usually first-person, even though your version of an event may be different from that of a sibling with the same experiences. People read life stories primarily for entertainment and inspiration.

Both forms can be difficult to read unless they have tension or creative conflict holding the entire piece together. The best ones have a thread running through them, connecting all the parts, just like a picture puzzle has a main focus. People want meaningful reading, not just accounts of one trip, music concert, or car purchase after another. Biography should be as close to a novel as possible, but true to the facts. It aims to show the essence of the subject, while autobiography aims to show yourself as an authentic person. Readers will recognize it as a subjective interpretation of your life.

I recommend avoiding a grocery list of dates and events in both types of writing. Don't include everything you've discovered about another person or even yourself. It may be difficult to leave out a wonderful meeting with an old friend, or the time you shook hands with the president of the United States, but is it important to your main thought? Put the unused material in a file labeled "precious moments" and leave it there for the children to discover after you're gone.

Memoir: In common usage, the terms "memoir" and "autobiography" are interchangeable. Technically, however, a memoir emphasizes your particular view of life, often during a particular period. It forces you to select a few experiences and to give them shape and order. A memoir is often about a selected portion of your life, to show the patterns that emerged over time. William Zinsser, in *Inventing the Truth: The Art and Craft of Memoir*, writes that the memoir, unlike the autobiography, assumes the details of one's life – that you were born, went to school, and so forth. It bypasses these to focus on a specific section of your story. It gives a window into your life experiences.

I think about memoir writing as allowing someone else to peek through a keyhole to learn how you experienced life at a certain time. A keyhole won't give you the big picture, just a small part. You are looking at your experiences from the viewpoint of a more mature understanding to help you and your readers find sense through the telling. You are looking for the key to access your interior life, what made you tick, and what made you the person you are today.

Reminiscences, recollections, stories, photos, etc.: You could write a series of vignettes about your life, not necessarily connected by broad themes, or collect family stories and compile them into a book. One Christmas, I gave children and friends a small book of photocopied stories I had collected over the years: *Into the Twilight Zone: Stories My Father and Others Told Me Too Good to Throw Out.* I enjoyed putting it together. Now I know those stories are safe from being forgotten. I plan to keep adding more as I find them.

Collection of letters or journal entries: Many life stories are composed entirely of selected and edited excerpts from old letters and journals.

Scrapbook or album: Call it "The Seasons of My Life." Divide your life into 12 periods, labeling each one by a month. If each month represents seven years of your life, January would represent your preschool years, February your early school years, and so forth. Write a story about something that happened in your family or to you in each "month." Add old photos of yourself as a baby, or of your parents. What was your favorite food as a young child? Did you have a bedtime prayer? Table prayers? What about some songs or games? In the April of your life, you could write about courtship and marriage. If you are good at scrapbooking, here's a chance to shine.

Cookbook album: This can be about anything related to food and family. One year, I gave my children a collection of favorite family recipes and copies of their childhood writings. I called it "Soul Food." They devoured it.

Video: Include photos, video clips, interviews, narration, and music to give a visual picture of your life or that of a loved one.

Confession: "I Was a Teenage Hippie" would be a tell-all account of a particularly emotional part of your life that you have been secretive about until now.

Before you continue, decide the audience for this planned manuscript: yourself, your family, or a broader audience. That decision will determine the form and content of your writing. Little children need something simpler than adults. People unfamiliar with the scientific language of a chemist may be turned off by a manuscript with details of your significant research in that area.

Choice of audience guides you in deciding what to include. A broad audience won't know who "Gerald" is. Your immediate family will know he's your brother. A broad audience doesn't need or want a lot of insignificant detail. Perhaps your family doesn't, either. Always remember you don't have to tell your reader every time you brushed your teeth or filled the car with gas.

After you have gathered considerable material and have a fair idea about what you plan to do, write a statement to yourself that explains your purpose to yourself. I have sometimes taped this statement to my computer as I write to keep it in mind. It will keep you on track. Experienced writers learn to do this in their minds. Example: "I am writing my life story to show why I changed from being a teacher to a car salesman."

In my book *The Storekeeper's Daughter*, I showed how my experiences as an immigrant's daughter forced me to deal with two cultures: Canadian and Russian-German. My parents, although wanting to become Canadian, were firmly attached to some old-country ways. I wanted to wear the same kinds of clothes as my friends. Mother was reluctant to have us wear shorts and slacks, Dad even more so. No men's clothing on his daughters! Movies were another taboo. The first time I went to a movie in the city and looked at the star-studded ceiling of the theater, I felt transported into a fairyland, while at the same time hoping I would not be struck dead for the great sin I was committing.

Theme is another aspect of writing. An overarching theme helps you to see your life as a whole rather than in little bits. A jigsaw puzzle gives you the advantage of being able to look at the picture on the cover to reorient yourself each time you work at it. The theme of a puzzle about a big green field with cows grazing in the foreground and fluffy clouds floating overhead might be the beauty of rural life. You wouldn't usually find Mickey Mouse in a go-cart chasing across the landscape. He would destroy the unity of the picture.

A theme keeps you from wandering all over your life without purpose. I wrote a book about my widowhood and how I came to terms with being a single mother supporting four young children in *Alone: A Widow's Search for Joy*. I could have included all kinds of material about my life at the time, but I stuck with issues related to widowhood. Family histories often also have themes.

Think through your feelings as you work with your material. It may take a while. You are trying to convey feelings through facts and events. The hardest part may be acknowledging that you had such strong feelings at one time. To write *The Storekeeper's Daughter*, I had to acknowledge my inner conflict caused by living in an immigrant home.

WRITING OPTION:

Write a possible opening paragraph for your manuscript after choosing one of the above structural types. The opening paragraph is often the most important in the book. It either draws the readers into your writing or turns them off. Forget about starting with, "A bouncing baby boy was born to George and Vera Plotzky in northern Minnesota on May 19, 1932."

In my autobiography, I began:

> I stepped off the train at the Winnipeg Canadian National Railways station and looked around anxiously – or was it eagerly? Would there be someone to meet me as promised? Night was falling on this Thursday evening in late August. I had arrived from Saskatoon, Saskatchewan, where I had been working as a legal secretary for the last few years.

I hope it draws you to the complete story.

GETTING
STARTED WRITING
ABOUT YOURSELF

I've often been asked, in more than 30 years of teaching personal writing, how to get started. As I do when starting a jigsaw puzzle, I begin by looking for the edge pieces, the boundaries of a life. I refer to this early stage as "softening the soil of memory." Compare it to digging up a patch of the heavily-walked path from the house to the barn of your childhood home. What happened on that path in addition to walking?

Where will you find information to write about yourself?

1.   Memory is the first and main resource, so learn to tap that resource. Your memory is better than you think. It just needs stimulation. We need cues to help us remember the details. Start with incidents you

remember well, which probably will be those with high emotional impact. Memory is most accurate about such events.

What stories come to mind without much thought? Every family has favorite stories about a colorful personality – the ancestor who stowed away on a ship coming to the United States, the one who lived on bread and peanut butter while going to college, or the one who spent the night in jail one Halloween. In your own life, these memories may include the time you nearly drowned but were too embarrassed to holler for help, or when you got lost in a city. Work with these first. Place these stories in file folders according to your age at the time, and if you haven't got a filing cabinet, find a cardboard box that fits.

2.   Talk to relatives and friends about yourself and your family. Write them letters with a list of questions you want answered. Get them involved in your project. Your enthusiasm will stir interest in exploring your family's story.

> A few decades ago my siblings and I spent an afternoon trying to top each other's stories about our growing up in a small Saskatchewan community. Each memory prompted another. At the end of the afternoon, we decided these stories were too good to forget so my brother offered to edit a book of our stories. The result was a self-published book, *Growing Up in Blaine Lake by Five Who Did*. I treasure that volume of memories.

3. Sort through old naturalization papers, military records, census records, church records, old maps, letters, journals, school yearbooks, newspapers, and photograph albums. You are looking for more than just names and dates. You are tracking down details and stories connected with events and material related to their context. What was happening in the community and broader world as you were growing up? Use the Internet to find dates of elusive events in world history. As you study old photographs, take a close look at clothing, furnishings, and decorations to determine the social level of your family.

4. Check the Internet to find news articles and obituaries of family members. Some significant dates may be listed in the family Bible.

   At one level, you are looking for bits of information about dates, places, names, and events to form the edge or border of your life puzzle. At another level, you will take these pieces of information and make a whole out of them. You want to turn statistics into real human beings who experienced joys and sorrows, successes and failures.

5. Visit church, county, and local historical libraries. Librarians are there to help you.

6. Locate family treasures and heirlooms. Ask why these artifacts were kept. What is the story behind them?

7.   Visit cemeteries to search for tombstones with family information. Make rubbings of cemetery markers or copy all information carefully. When you see a large number of deaths, particularly children's deaths in many families in the same year, this may be a clue to an epidemic and why some distant relative died as a child.

> In the small town of Kronsweide in the Ukraine, our tour group visited what was once an old Mennonite cemetery. In the less-used portion of the cemetery, we saw a few old broken gravestones inscribed with German names, nearly buried in the underbrush and weeds. In this area my father, as a young man and oldest male in the family, had buried four close adult relatives, including his father, within two weeks. All had died of typhus in 1920 following the Russian Revolution. The experience of having to tear down fences to make coffins, to find a cart to transport them to the cemetery, and to say the final prayer at the gravesite alone, left him scarred for life. I thought of my father's pain and that of the many others who dragged starved bodies in makeshift coffins to this place, as I stumbled over the rough terrain.

8.   Read biographies and autobiographies of people who lived through similar experiences as yours. Read histories of the eras you lived through. *The Worst Hard Time: The Untold Story of Those Who Survived the Great American Dust Bowl* by Timothy

Egan is a great resource if you or your parents made it through the Dust Bowl of western Kansas and the Oklahoma Panhandle. Such reading will give you an understanding of your family, not just as a unit, but as a people living in a larger context of world events, natural disasters, and political maneuvering. Read about the times you and your family lived in until you feel the strain in your back as you think about your grandfather digging stumps to clear the land.

Remember, you are making something new. Not everything needs to be preserved on paper. Some details can be suppressed, but for the time being, save everything you discover about yourself. You are putting down on paper what your life has been.

I often begin a class with one or more of the following six exercises. These may take weeks and months to complete, but they are a good beginning because they make you familiar and comfortable with the sweep of your own life.

EXERCISE 1

Make a list of all stories that come to mind quickly and easily – all kinds, all subjects, all time periods. Keep adding to this list.

This is the most important of all the exercises, for it eventually will give you an overview of your life. On a large, and I mean large, sheet of paper, draw eight vertical lines, labeling each division with a life stage. Either take your age and divide it by eight or look for natural divisions in your life story, such as birth to kindergarten, grade school, high school, and college. The last division starts with where you are now. At the top of each column, identify each time division by date and your age at the time. Eight is not a magic number, but it works. Use nine divisions, even 10, if you have to.

Next, dig for a few words that describe the main qualities of your life during each period. I've had students describe the first period, child-hood, as "blissful," and "carefree," but also "miserable," "unhappy," and "frightening." One woman said it had been dreadfully lonely. Another talked about her early childhood as hurtful because of the mean names her mother called her.

Then, under each period, list the main events, as you remember them, which support the words you used to describe it. If you were unhappy during this period, you might list that during grade school your family moved three times, a baby brother was added to the fam-ily, your father lost his job, you had the measles and lost your favorite pet. You are supporting your generalization with details. This list gives you something to write about.

If you prefer, use a metaphor to describe each period. When my children were all small, I felt like a mother hen. I was feeding, changing, and clucking over them all day long.

> My writing class was surprised when I listed "lonely" for early married life. My new husband and I had moved far from my home community in the Canadian prairies to a small community on the West Coast where German was the preferred language of daily discourse. I spoke it hesitantly. My husband was immediately drawn into teaching duties. We didn't have a car, and I knew no one. Women did not work outside the home. I was lonely, desperately lonely. I missed the heady stimulation of college life. When I admitted my feelings, other women in class acknowledged they had felt the same in early married life. Sometimes it is hard to admit you had certain feelings. When you do, you will find others identifying with you.

Under each of your categories, write the roles you played during each period: child, student, spouse, parent, wage-earner, grandparent, retiree, member of the military, volunteer.

List the main events in your life during each period: school, piano lessons, trips to the zoo or the doctor.

Add to these the turning points in each period (decisions or happenings that forced a change in your life). What changed? These are sometimes sickness, moves, deaths, or returning to school as an adult.

What were some firsts you remember? First funeral and death, first travel from home, first hamburger, first arousal of sexual feelings and experimentations, and first religious stirrings. Think also of your first major illness, radio, television, employment, unemployment, lack of money, or a fight and reconciliation. The list is endless.

Add objects and places in each of the divisions that had lasting interest: paper dolls, bicycles, books, a jackknife, a skating rink, a swimming pool, an empty lot next door, pop music, or boys.

You will find that the memories of smell are strong. What kinds of smells do you think of for each period? Sounds? Tastes? Colors? Activities? Objects of significance? Recall the smell of chalk buried in sawdust in small wooden boxes, oiled floors, and sweaty bodies after recess. Coax and prod your memory. Move slowly through an event to evoke details.

Under each period, list several people who interested you greatly or were associated with intense emotion, such as the doctor who came to the house, a neighbor, a school bully.

What was happening in the larger world, such as the Wall Street crash of 1929, wars, conscription, rationing, strikes, elections, parades, and riots?

Another category might be defining moments, such as taking piano lessons, refusing to get involved with the wrong group of friends, standing up for something you believe in, maybe yielding to a temptation to steal or cheat.

Keep adding to this chart the following: Births of siblings, playmates, family discipline, religious training, chores, games, home remedies, odd people, illnesses, family celebrations, typical Sundays, family moves, and deaths. You can trace these and other items over your lifetime to show how they have changed. Always ask yourself how you felt at the time. How did this affect my family? What happened as a result?

You eventually will have a huge grid of your whole life with many details, enough to write a chapter or more about each life stage, with possibly the theme already identified by the initial words, so start with a big sheet of paper. The important thing is to be honest with yourself. Don't write what you think your readers expect you to write. You want to get as close to the truth as possible. Authenticity is the goal. (I will refer to this grid throughout the book.)

EXERCISE 3

Draw a floor plan of a house where you lived a long time or where you had some significant experiences. Add the furniture in outline form and, alongside, list events that happened in the various rooms as they come to you.

You might also draw a map of the farm, city block, or village where you lived, identifying the people in each house. Trace your path from your house to school or some other place you went to frequently, and note what you saw and heard along the way.

> This idea came to me when I realized how important
> it was to my father to have in his hands a carefully drawn
> map of the village of Rosental in the Ukraine, where he

had grown up. It showed the main street with the store where he worked, the house where his parents had lived, and the mill his father operated, as well as other landmarks that returned him to his carefree life as a child of the Russian steppes. That village map helped me later, when I was researching stories he had told us about his childhood. Together with my brother, I began outlining the streets of Blaine Lake, Saskatchewan, where we had grown up, and identifying neighbors, business establishments, churches, and other main landmarks. The process brought back many memories.

EXERCISE 4

You are the scavenger of facts and stories related to yourself and your family over several generations. Develop a family timeline that gives a historical overview of your family, beginning with the earliest date. By a timeline, I simply mean a line with dates on one side and a list of events on the other. Think of these events as signposts along your family's journey. What historical events did your family live through? Where were they when these events happened? All these events shaped the family. Such a timeline gives you an overview of your family.

Keep the grid of your life and the timeline somewhere convenient and keep adding details as you come across them in their research.

Count on the Internet as your ally to find elusive facts, dates, and events about major world events that intersected with your life. Look for evidence of the following factors.

Migrations: Other than Native Americans, every American family came from some place other than the United States a generation or more ago. Where was that country? Maybe they also moved from state to state or from one side of a city to the other. Farm-to-city and vice versa is another kind of move. Why did they migrate or move and when? What stories were passed down about those moves? This gives you background information about yourself.

Wars: Who went to war, who stayed home, and why? What happened as a result?

Economic hardships and successes, such as stock market crashes, the Depression era, the Dust Bowl, crop failures, boom crops, foot and mouth disease in cattle, promotions, inheritances, etc.

Social changes in attitudes toward family, sexuality, women's roles, race, etc.

Technological changes such as the advent of the automobile, airplanes, electricity, mechanized farm equipment, appliances, and medicine.

Disasters or other misfortunes such as tornadoes, floods, fire, burglaries, crime encounters, bankruptcies.

Changes in means of earning livelihood, workplace, and type of work

Changes in religious affiliation

Major travel

Call this your Personal Information Sheet. It may take several weeks to complete, but once it's done you can keep referring to it when you need information. Use this as a guide, and put your answers on full sheets of paper. Hint: You can also use this to write your own obituary.

Given name	
Birth: place, date, parents' full names, including your mother's maiden name, and any unusual circumstances at your birth	
Siblings: their birth dates, marriages, deaths, and names of children	
Education: grade school, high school, college, other institutions	
Marriages, deaths, divorces: including dates, names, and places	
Children: full names and nicknames, dates, where born, marriages and names of their spouse(s) and children	
Work history and positions held: Make a timeline of all the places you worked	
Military experience	
Major geographic moves: List dates and places you lived over the years	
Unusual experiences: such as robberies and accidents	

Organizations you belonged to and positions held	
Church membership, activities, and organizations	
Volunteer activities throughout life	
Travel, special vacations	
Awards, honors, professional accomplishments	
Famous people in your life	
Close friends	
Life achievements: official and unofficial	
Publications	
Special skills, interests, hobbies	
Foreign language skills	
Main character traits: Don't be bashful here. What legacy would you like to leave behind?	
Life challenges	
Banners and bandwagons: What values did you hold high?	
Political views	

What would you add to your list?

EXERCISE 6

Develop a simple family tree of five to six generations. Add dates as you discover them. Look for two sources for each date. Be aware that spellings of names may change through the decades.

This family tree will help you identify people as relatives talk about them. Keep your family tree close at hand when you interview relatives. Always keep track of where you got the information so that you can check it later as needed. *Keep family lines separate.* Keep each story separate so that you can file it later on.

Generation 1 – your maternal or paternal grandparents

Generation 2 – your parent and his/her siblings

Generation 3 – you and your siblings and spouses

Generation 4 – your children

Generation 5 – your children's children and spouses

Generation 6 – your great-grandchildren and spouses

When you have completed these six exercises, you will have made a substantial beginning. You now have most of the edge, or border pieces, of your life's puzzle. The biggest hurdle for many would-be writers is to keep writing interest high. It helps to have a goal: a small finished album of pictures and writings by Christmas next year, or something like that, to give to children and grandchildren.

Look for a writing group in your vicinity to keep you encouraged. Make a date with yourself for two mornings a week at a certain time. Forget dishes and laundry, golf and TV programs, anything that keeps you from your assigned spot at the computer.

You've lived a long, full life. Writing a life history won't get done in a few months. So plan for a place to work and materials to work with. Invest in file folders. A loose-leaf notebook also works in the beginning but don't use a bound notebook. Always write on one side only so you can move pages around.

WRITING OPTION:

Write about one story that comes to mind easily. Maybe it's about the time your brother, Jimmie, got lost in a large department store, or the day the family went camping for the first time together and a bear got into your food. Maybe it is some event like your father getting sick and losing his job so that the older children all had to go to work to support the family.

WRITING ABOUT OTHER PEOPLE

Some people get hung up on politics or stamp collecting or restoring old cars. I've got this thing about people's stories. I'm always telling older adults to write down their own and other people's experiences — if not for their own benefit, then for a future biographer, historical society, or their own children.

Not everyone understands why. Why immortalize in print the many little events that make up a person's life? If life had meaning for one person, an account of that life will have meaning for others. People are desperately looking for meaning, not just something to fill the hours in their scramble through life.

A family historian, biographer, or memoirist is able to separate the elements of a person's life that have meaning beyond immediate family and friends, and outside the little community where the person lived. When a writer discovers the soul of a person, that biographer discovers the person. And that will have meaning for readers.

Dr. Mary Verghese was a doctor to lepers in India many decades ago. We have few lepers in America, so ordinarily her life would have little significance for Americans. However, her biographer, Dorothy Clarke Wilson, showed through the details of her ministry to lepers in India a faith in God that surmounted obstacles that would make most people call out, "Lord, I quit." After an accident that left Dr. Verghese paralyzed from the waist down, she said, "Lord, take my hands." She operated on lepers' hands while sitting down. The title of the book is *Take My Hands*.

I read it at a time when I was floundering in the bitter darkness of sorrow brought on by my young husband's death and the need to make big changes in my life. I had little to give God except my love for language. I said to God, "Take my words" and began a writing ministry that has lasted more than 40 years. But a biography inspired me.

Nothing can equal stories of actual people. The difference between the autobiographer and the biographer is simple – one focuses on the significance of his or her own life, the other on the significance of another's. Both highlight what motivated a person to travel down a certain path.

Modern biography dates from the time of the First World War. Up to that time, only the novelist was allowed to deal with characters as humans with flaws and faults among their strengths. The biographer was expected to present an established image of a person's reputation with no blemishes.

A new tone of realism crept into the novels around the time of World War I. Soldiers in that war were the first who could afford the moral luxury of admitting to fear under combat. The writers of life histories adopted this new freedom, showing their main characters not as flawless heroes, faultless leaders, or those who always conquered every foe.

The life story of Eleanor Roosevelt is a fascinating account of a woman who suffered immeasurably as a child because her mother thought she was homely and told her so, according to her biographer. She overcame these odds as well as difficulties in her marriage to Franklin Delano Roosevelt to become an important world leader in her own right. Without biographers, we would never have known the inside story.

Why Write a Biography?

1. **To teach the art of living.**

    Truth is stronger than fiction. If the first purpose of literature generally is to teach the art of living, autobiography and biography does it directly. Someone shows by one person's life: "This is the way it worked for this individual."

    I have often told audiences, "Why hang onto your life after you have lived it? Give it away." If it contains even the smallest truth that may inspire, enrich, and ennoble, then hand it over to the next generation. When I write about my father, I want readers to catch a glimpse of his generous nature despite the difficulties he endured as a child. I want readers to see the spark, the inner light, that drove him.

A good biography should be interesting to read. As someone said, "It should not read like Washington looks on the dollar bill – awesomely noble, but kind of stuffed."

Good biographies benefit readers so that they can say, "This book had something in it for me at this time in life." Biographies show courage in action, with the subject overcoming adversity and gaining wisdom and willingness to change their opinions and attitudes. A biography is not just a series of events with birth and death as its boundaries. In biography, you get answers to life.

2.   **To commemorate or honor a parent or grandparent, other relative or friend, church or community leader.**

Greatness is not limited to the rich and famous. It is a trait found abundantly in mothers and fathers, teachers, neighbors, and friends. Look for it in a person's stories about courage, love, and enduring. You want to make the reader realize the subject is worth knowing about.

Main Characteristics of Biography

1.   **It's individualized.** It should not be possible to write your subject's sibling's name over it.

2. **It's true.** As a biographer, you are a historian. Your writing should be based on personal experience and research, not hearsay. It should be a faithful picture of a human being on his or her way through life. You do not make up facts to fit your thesis about the person. Work from primary materials, if possible, such as letters, journals, and interviews with people who knew the person. Memory is important, but it can be fallible and biased. Journalists look for at least two sources for every fact.

You may be tempted to idealize, distort, even over-dramatize to make the person's character fit your predetermined image of them. Don't rush to highlight with spicy and gossipy details, or to debunk and make the character a dunce if you didn't like him or her.

Problems arise when your initial evaluation turns out to be false after careful research. You will have to come to terms with the conflict in yourself if you viewed your father as a saintly man, only to find out he was a philanderer, bringing much sorrow to your mother. Check and double-check each detail. If the person is still living, tread lightly around material that may open you to libel. You don't want someone's lawyer coming after you with a subpoena.

On the other hand, you may be tempted to record only the subject's big deeds or exploits rather than include everyday events. Don't be overawed by your subject and make him or her one-sided.

Another danger is to chronologically grind through the person's life from birth to death, detail by detail: "Then, and then, and then ...." Most writers of biographies point out that no life is complete without childhood. The child is the parent of the adult, so you want to include something of the person's early years. You might ask, "Why did this shy and socially inept child growing up in the backwoods become a powerful church leader or politician? What were the turning points in his or her life? What did life do to her? What did he do to life?" Recognize that when you highlight certain traits in your subject, you reveal what you value in another person.

If you are ambivalent about your feelings toward your subject, become familiar enough with him or her that you learn to like and respect the person. While it is not necessary to tell everything, what is told must be true so that your readers don't shelve your whole manuscript because they know some of it isn't true.

Master your material. Work from primary materials if possible, such as first-hand experience, letters, journals, and interviews with people who knew the person. A modern difficulty is that no one today writes what one can call real letters – the kind a biographer would turn cartwheels for. I worry what future biographers will do when they find old computer discs that no longer match their more advanced equipment.

Once you get a good start on your material, select a major theme on the basis of your audience. Weave in the main conflicts in the person's life. You need that element just like you need it in a short story or novel. Make the reader want to turn to the next page. The tension in the person's life may not be immediately clear to you, but keep looking. You are trying to show the progressive development of that person's discovery of the world. Someone has said, "A person must have fought something, fought for something, or with something – perhaps with the Devil, with his own soul. Life that possesses no conflict possesses no victory."

Your character may never have methodically worked out a philosophy of life, but if you keep digging you will find what made the person tick. As I wrote my late husband's biography, *Born Out of Season*, I realized more and more that he lived by a truth his father had told him when he was young: "It is better to spend 50 years struggling for the truth and making mistakes than to live for a short time according to tradition." He also quoted this advice from his father: "If you can do something that no one else can do, then don't do what everyone else is doing. Aim to develop your unique gift." He spent a short lifetime pursuing a dream of a vocation in religious journalism, a new field in our church world at that time.

What liberties can you take in biography, or autobiography for that matter? Don't reconstruct long and involved conversations. These often end up sounding stilted and obviously included just to pass on information. Let the subject speak primarily from diaries, journals, letters, and similar materials. Brief conversations are acceptable. Interpret available facts with care and support them solidly. If your uncle was a good-for-nothing, how do you know this?

Choose your attitude toward your material, whether detached observer, or warm, friendly sympathetic family member. I couldn't write about someone I didn't have respect and sympathy for, so my biographies have been about relatives such as my husband, my mother, and several aunts who endured unspeakable hardships while exiled to hard labor in northern Siberia after World II; Sister Frieda Kauffman, who spearheaded the establishment of the deaconess movement through the Bethel Deaconess Hospital and Home in Newton, Kansas; and others. As you write, avoid passing judgment on your subject, for or against. Don't preach sermons about the sins you see in this person. Let their story show their life.

In writing a biography, you can choose from several forms. In the critical form, you always remain present in the story, telling the reader what to think, as "the records tell us ..." or "it is probable that ...." The narrative form may appeal to you more. For a more informal biography, don't flood the reader with documentation. Add that at the end. Omit what is redundant. Simply tell the story of your subject's life and let the readers make their own judgment. The following story is written solely from personal experience over several years with an older friend.

When I returned from a week-long trip in 1985, I learned that my valued friend, Esther Hiebert Ebel, had died. Not unexpectedly. She had been ill off and on for months. Before I left, I visited her for a short while, praying her suffering would end soon.

I can't recall when our friendship started. Probably I went to her for information about her early life, for she was a bottomless well of information about early times in the our small community, the church, and the college where I taught. She had lived in Hillsboro, Kansas, all her life, first as the daughter of a prominent churchman, then as the wife of a Tabor College professor, and, later, as dean of women at Tabor. She was always a faithful member of her church.

I considered her a friend and mentor. She took me into her life as she reminisced about what it had been like to grow up, marry, and work in the church. Yet none of the tensions arising from quickly changing times left her bitter or discouraged. Her loyalty to Christ and the church were greater than taking satisfaction in mulling through pettiness in relationships or unnecessarily harsh church regulations. She encouraged my endeavors in support of women and took interest in my family. Their needs became her prayer items.

Esther was concerned about personal righteousness before God. Occasionally, she mentioned she had had to take herself "behind the woodshed" because of discouragement, loneliness, or worries. Sometimes her self-chastisement was for reasons I thought unnecessary, but she knew when attitudes were defeating her, and she felt convicted. She wanted nothing between God and herself.

She made it a rule never to speak unkindly of another person, or to be upset by something she couldn't change. If I commented that I would find annoying the regular flushing of toilets in adjoining apartments, her only response was "I don't hear them." For her the noise did not exist because it was a part of life she couldn't change.

She maintained an active visitation ministry to residents of the Salem Hospital and Home where she lived. When she had strength, she wrote letters to her many friends and "adopted" grandchildren, and sewed small items for gifts, for relief organizations, for the mission circle, and to meet individual needs.

One evening when I arrived, she was making pieced lap robes for nursing home residents (and few women could piece quilt blocks as accurately as she), so the next time I came I brought along a box of tailor's samples I had picked up at the local thrift store. As we sat and sorted, to our dismay we found the box contained a mixture of textiles, colors, and sizes of blocks.

"This project will prove too big a headache," I suggested. "Let's forget it." She didn't give in. We laid out one lap robe that evening, matching colors and textiles as best we could.

Later that summer, her car rolled into my driveway, an unusual event, and she stepped out, looking very pleased, car–rying a large box which she presented to me. She had pieced the multi–sized, multi–colored, and multi–textured blocks into a quilt for me instead of lap robes for the residents.

Inside was a note: "Dear Katie, I have pieced covers of wool, cotton, and synthetic fabrics and always had uniform pieces. Here was a new challenge: a mixture of textiles and four sizes of patches. Surely these pieces can be arranged in some design to make harmony in a cover without bulges and wrinkles. One day I discovered myself in the patch-work of the varied textiles. I look at this quilt cover and see myself as a patch that fits into the fabric of Salem Home and Apartments. Yes, we are of different shapes and sizes, yet there is harmony through acceptance and willingness to be trimmed to fit into the spot we are to fit."

The quilt articulates her life motto: a willingness to fit in. After that event, her living space became more and more restricted as her health deteriorated. One lengthy illness followed another. Each brief recovery made it more difficult to find joy to return to life, especially when she found herself tethered to an oxygen tank and her voice weakening and eyesight dimming.

"Give me something to think about" was her most frequent request. "Talk about what you're doing." I found her sometimes playing Boggle with herself to keep her mind occupied with "good thoughts." Now I had to initiate the prayer time with which we often ended our little sessions.

The previous spring after Memorial Day we had driven to several cemeteries to retrieve the wreathes she had placed where her closest relatives were buried so she could use them again next year. She was the faithful keeper of the memories of the departed. Each time I recall her life I lay a wreath anew to her memory and hope others will lay one down beside it. She taught by life and word that there can be "harmony without bulges."

After additional research, the above paragraphs became the basis for a much longer biography of Esther Ebel's life that was published in a historical periodical.

Important Sources to Investigate

1. Read all that has been written about your subject and also about the socio-historical period in which he or she lived. If your character lived through World War I, find out about this first great war to end all wars. Don't forget obituaries.

2. Look for material that has never been made public. One class member told us that she had recently discovered a stack of letters her father had written to his first wife. Should she read them? "Yes," we said. Photocopy such materials first, to have a second copy available, and then read them.

3. If possible, visit the places associated with your subject's life. In 1989, I was privileged to travel to the Ukraine to visit the place my parents had lived in their early married life. I found the spot, high on a hill, where the Funk windmill had once stood. I walked the street of the store my father had worked in, and I stood at the edge of the ravine his father had stumbled into when the revolutionary soldiers shot at him. I prefer this to traveling to Palestine to visit the places where Jesus may have walked. I find more immediacy.

4.   Interview people who knew your subject. Look for discrepancies in the material. I had my mother's and my father's versions of how my father, newly-wed, had found my mother's family after they had been lost in the Russian Revolution. In Moscow, I interviewed a newly-discovered aunt, now well into her 80s, for her version. In Canada, I interviewed a younger aunt for what she had to say about this traumatic event. Their stories agreed in remarkable ways.

Look for small details that will make your character human, such as gestures, and hair and eye color. Look for facts about people, their affiliations, actions, and beliefs. Look for facts about places. What did the streets of your hometown look like in 1918? What did people eat and drink at that time? Did your mother wear a size 6 petite or was she size 20XL? Those few figures tell the reader a lot. For the story about finding my mother's family, her red hair was an important detail, because my father was looking for her father, who also had red hair.

WRITING TIP:

If you plan to write about your father, first, as quickly as possible, list all the details, events, and ideas you can remember about him, in any order. Keep going over your list and adding details to details. This is called looping.

Next, sort all the details according to similar subject matter. Put all details that describe him in one column, and all details about his work in another. Then, organize your lists into some logical order. Now you can begin a first draft.

This short writing about my father is a brief example of what you can do. I wrote a longer one in my books Good Times with Old Times *and* The Storekeeper's Daughter. *In writing about him, I looked for details that, grouped together, would show a character trait.*

When I think of my father, I see him striding to work in his tan-colored smock in the morning. He never ambled or sauntered. That was not his style. There was work to do, work he loved to do, and he was heading toward it. For about 40 years, he managed or owned a grocery store. He had a strong sense of being the wage earner of the family, his job as a husband and father; it was Mother's to manage the household and keep us all happy. Not always was he able to provide as he would have liked to, but he worked hard to supply his family with its needs, and more if he could.

He had a strange fear of banks, brought over from the old country, compounded by the failure of banks in 1929. Although he used the local bank for his store business, he never had a personal account as far as I can remember or wrote personal checks. His method of doing personal business was cash, which he carried in wads in his pockets, sometimes pinned shut. In his later years, when he became forgetful, occasionally he took this wad out to count in full view of others to the horror of my sisters who witnessed his strange behavior. Once he paid a doctor bill in the 1930s for my sister's appendicitis surgery with cash, only several years later, when the deceased doctor's estate was settled, to be billed for it again. Our home was in upheaval for several days. He had no receipt and no paid check to back up his claim that he had paid the bill. Yet he knew he had paid it. He paid all bills. He was an honest man who believed in living within his means. He paid it again.

He was also always at the head of the line of anything, whether it was at a sideshow at a fair or to develop plans for assisting the destitute in our little village through relief programs in the hungry 1930s. He couldn't pass a hungry hobo who drifted into town without handing him something or sending him to the house with a note for Mother to give him a meal.

I also see his impatience with getting things done, whether by himself or with others. Careful craftsmanship was not his strength. When he built something, such as a teeter–totter for us children, the goal was speed, not beauty, so paint sometimes got slapped onto a board with great hurry and gusto. When we children worked for him in the store, he expected us to keep hustling, and if there was no business, to arrange cans on shelves – to look busy.

Yes, I can see him now at work at his accounts. He was a whiz with figures and a pencil, rapidly adding long columns, stopping to wet the pencil tip before going on to the next column. It was a pattern. He also had a pattern for getting ready for bed. First, he turned off the radio, checked the heater and doors, pulled the clock chain to lift the weights, and lastly, turned off the lights, even if we children were still reading, before heading upstairs. As I review his life, I see many habits, but especially patterns of being a caring man.

Should you let your subject read your material after you have written? This is debatable. Simple courtesy would dictate you should let them read it for factual accuracy. I've had family members read my biographies to check if I have the right slant or balance of ideas and facts.

WRITING OPTION:

Make a list of five people, living or dead, you would like to write about, who are worth writing about, and who might be possible to write about. Pick one person. What specific facet of that person's personality interests you? Talk to at least two or three people about that person before you get started.

CHOOSE A THEME AND PLOT

Going back over our lives as we get older is a normal process. It helps us achieve a better sense of the life cycle and to accept it with hope. It encourages us to determine legacies, both material and spiritual, how to live the rest of life, and to pass on information and wisdom. But above all, it gives us a grasp of the pattern of our lives. How to identify this pattern?

Consider the following scenario: The story of one man's life includes 16 DUI arrests, several domestic abuse situations, frequent job losses, and two divorces. What generalization can you make about his life? What is the thread running through his life?

Consider another scenario: A young girl from a poor home finds a way to get a high school and college education despite odds. Then she goes on to become an outstanding nurse, and, later, a wife, mother, and civic leader. She is a prominent figure in her church. What is the pattern in this story?

In working with your material over the course of months and years, you will discover a thread running through it, sometimes clearly visible, sometimes faint. You will see emerging patterns of thinking, speaking, and doing. Sometimes this awareness comes slowly, but wait for it, it will surely come.

One of my first students in a memoir writing class knew immediately what she was going to write about: growing up in a family of 12 children with all its problems and blessings. Ideas poured out of her because she knew her subject matter intimately.

In my family's early story, one dominant theme is the effect of a harsh communist government on its citizens living in the Soviet Union. Stories of brutality, hardship, suffering, and response to suffering has dominated my family's and my branch of our church denomination's history, alongside amazing stories of faith and trust in God. My family's history would not be complete without mention of this theme. However, not all themes are as clearly visible as in my case. So what do you do?

Remember, a theme is the underlying truth or principle of your writing. Think of the autobiography of any well-known person, and you will find a central theme running through it. You can match the theme of your life to classic themes such as good versus reality of evil; rags to riches; overcoming odds; the search for beauty, truth, and culture; the intense desire to bring about peace or justice; a quest for faith and belief; serving church and community; service to humanity; getting ahead in business or education or farming; overcoming a physical, educational, or social handicap; staying ahead of the Joneses; the quest to own ever more land and houses; striving to become a prize-winning quilter; living in a dysfunctional family; rearing a child with a disability; overcoming racial prejudice; or being a caregiver over a long period.

The theme may also be as simple as trying to be a decent person throughout life or to show how a special series of circumstances or a certain philosophy of life shaped your life. Like mining for diamonds, the search for a theme may be difficult but rewarding.

When I knit or crochet, I like to see a picture of what I am making. Before you can build a human life after God's pattern, you need to know what that pattern looks like. The Bible tells us about love, joy, peace, patience, and so forth, but the stories where these virtues are lived out are remembered better than the admonitions. We remember the New Testament story of the woman at the well and the blind beggar who was healed much better than the heavy sermons in the New Testament book of Romans. When you write your story or someone else's, you identify the pattern of your life and offer it to others to learn from.

Circumstances will always differ from those of your reader, but human emotions are the same now as they were in biblical days or your parent's time. Hope is always hope, love is always love, courage is always courage. My parents lived in a mud-plastered house; I live in a brick apartment building. Their floors were wood; mine are carpeted. They sat on hard benches and chairs, with nothing upholstered. I love my reclining rocker. They ate noodles and *Pracha Faat* (beggar's gravy). I like chicken and broccoli (really). I can't give my children stories about war and revolution like my parents gave me. But I can tell them stories that come out of my life.

I can write about my childhood disappointment at receiving an ugly purple vase in the school Christmas gift exchange. I can still see it vividly in my mind. It was probably something the money-poor family in the 1930s had in their home. I can write about wearing an old thin jacket all winter because I refused to wear my mother's old coat, altered to fit me. I can write about singing songs as a family in the old McLaughlin Buick, driving the long way to church early Sunday mornings.

Something always remains the same, regardless of the time period, and that is the emotions. All children feel the same about coming home to warmth and love. I rushed home every noon for years to a wonderful meal and Mother's welcoming smile. I do not know what it feels like to find a lost family, as my father did when he went looking for my mother's family lost in the Revolution, yet I recall my acute anxiety every time a child didn't come home on time in the late evening. I have never felt the fear of physical danger as my parents did during the Russian Revolution, but their stories have helped me understand despair at a senseless war and how to handle change and face uncertain odds.

No matter which generation tells the story, the feeling conveyed is important, and through the reader's identification with that emotion, they understand that pattern for living.

Family histories often also have themes or patterns if they are written in the form of a saga of generations. Some show how a man or woman dreamed big and then followed through on that dream with action – by moving to another country, establishing a homestead, starting a business, sacrificing to go to school, reaching for leadership opportunities – and then how succeeding generations picked up on these dreams.

When you write about your parents' and your dreams, you encourage your reader to dream not just about a bigger house or car but about the values worth preserving. You help the reader to create an image of the way another generation dreamed and made promises to God, church, and society, and of the way they risked, sometimes failed, and sometimes succeeded in keeping these promises.

My father came to Canada from Russia in 1923 with a dream for a better life for himself and his family. He told stories about the way it had been in the land of his birth. His stories were a way of giving us children roots by building strong memories.

A theme helps bring unity to your book. It keeps you from wandering all over the landscape. A jigsaw puzzle gives you the advantage of being able to look at the picture on the cover to reorient yourself each time you work at it. An awareness of a theme does the same.

To find the themes or truths in your life, keep going over the time-line or eight-division grid you made earlier. Ask relatives and friends what they think dominated your life or that of your family. You may be too close to the truth to recognize the overarching theme that pulls everything together into a whole. Instead, you are tempted to offer little bits, like confetti.

Think through your feelings as you work with your material. You are trying to convey feelings through facts and events. The hardest part may be acknowledging you had such feelings at one time. To write *The Storekeeper's Daughter*, I had to admit to myself that for a time I was unhappy not to have been born into a family of privilege with the means to send me on to college and sure success in life.

You have made huge progress in your writing, whether it is a short article about your father or a book-length manuscript, if you can state its theme in one simple sentence. If a friend asks, "What are you writing?" you have an answer: "I am planning to show how the various circumstances in my life led to my having the courage to enter the teaching profession and to stay with it for three decades." As you keep working with your material, keep asking yourself, "Have I still got my main focus clearly in sight?" It will keep you from chasing down rabbit paths when a new idea strikes you.

With a possible theme in mind, give your book a tentative title. I often come up with half a dozen before I settle on one. You can change it later on. Next, develop a simple outline. Give each chapter a tentative title and list the main stories you will include in it. Be prepared to move them around if need be. Everything is always open to revision. At this point, nothing is nailed down.

At what point in your life should you begin your actual story? Some writers begin at a turning point in life such as marriage, graduation from college, perhaps a sudden dismissal from a position, or at any point when emotions were intense. Then they use flashbacks to bring the reader up to date. You don't need to start with your birth.

The opening sentence is probably the most important in your book, for it either draws the reader into your material or causes her to drop the book in favor of something more interesting. Few people read out of duty these days. Take your readers by the hand and draw them into your material at once. Don't take too long to get into the heart of your subject. I've told many classes that you don't need to eat a whole egg to find out if it's good. One bite, one paragraph, will give you the flavor.

WRITING OPTION:

Write a short essay about what you see as the pattern of your life or the thread showing up all the way through it. In these paragraphs, explain to yourself what you see as the significant points in your life journey. It is important to see the full sweep of your life, not just isolated events, if you plan to write a longer manuscript. The main thing is to keep retrieving your life from the long-forgotten store of memories.

STORIES ARE ALWAYS WINNERS

The best way to connect with children and grandchildren is by telling stories. Adults like them too. Stories are for joining the past to the future, writes Tim O'Brien in *The Things They Carried*. The success of the *Chicken Soup for the Soul* books is based on the premise that people are attracted to stories. Stories are the glue that holds families together.

Storytelling is a common way of telling others about our lives: "I remember when I first learned to ride a bicycle," or "I watched with horror as a child when two adult men brawled on Main Street, curses and fists flying, noses bloody." By telling your story, you objectify your experience and separate yourself from it so that you can give it away. Knowing your own story, adds Rachel Naomi Remen in

Kitchen Table Wisdom, requires "a personal response to life, an inner experience of life. It is possible to live a life without experiencing it." The purpose of this book is to help you find your story, or how you responded to life.

I like to think of stories as a way of embracing the reader. When you share a personal story, you open yourself to the reader and say, "I trust you with my story." In our writing class, one member waited until the last day of the session to read her story of childhood hurt. She told us, "I waited until I was sure I trusted you." It took eight weeks of sharing stories before she felt we wouldn't judge her or her story.

When I was a beginning writer, my mother told me, "Katie, I want you to write the story of how Dad found my family lost during the Russian Revolution of 1917–19." I carried that mandate in my mind for several years, until I retired and had time for serious research. I held this story close to my heart for several years before I could share it publicly. Only when I trusted my audience, and later, readers, could I let this intimate part of our family's life go. It was published eventually in a shortened form in *The Storekeeper's Daughter* and in a longer form in *Journal of Mennonite Studies.*

What is the subject matter of
personal narrative or story?

Such narratives can be about a variety of personal experiences – Uncle Joe's attitude toward his gout, the hideous purse you bought at a garage sale thinking it was a Gucci, being stuck in traffic, the worst day of your life, a random act of kindness someone did for you, a random act of brutality you witnessed, an experience with prejudice, or hoping for a kiss on a date.

Point of view. Your personal viewpoint ("I") of what happened works best to find the truth or meaning from the experience if you are part of the story. When you use third person, referring to yourself by name throughout, you move the story a step away from yourself. You may have been told as a child that to use the first-person pronoun shows rudeness, but, believe me, it's OK to use it. But don't say, "Jane and myself left for the ballgame." "Mother gave it to Johnnie and I" is also incorrect!

How to start. Start a first draft of your story, boldly using the pronoun "I" as your first word. It will catapult you into the story at once. The final version may not begin with this word, but it helps to get you started. Write "I saw …, I did …, I gave …, I got lost …, I traveled to …" Now continue with the story, as fast as you can. After a day or two, come back to what you wrote and go over it again, adding details. After another week, do the same. Each time you rewrite, you will find more memories returning.

What makes a great story?

It must stir the soul, capture the heart, make us laugh, or even better, do all three. To be a memoir, it must be true, not fiction. The easiest stories have to do with our own experiences, what we hated, snubbed, loved, fought for, and treasured. Stories evoke in us "right-brain imagination, tenderness, and therefore wholeness," writes William Bausch in *Storytelling: Imagination and Faith.*

What is a story?

A story has to do with events in time, with life in motion. Sometimes the movement is in the inner life, not always action that can be observed externally. Something happens (an action) to someone (character) in place and time (setting), usually illustrating some comment or reaction to life (theme). A story should focus on a meaningful series of events, held together by some theme, so that when you're finished, the reader doesn't mutter, "So what?" A good narrative covers a unit of time, complete in itself, not just a fragment.

> One morning I drove downtown, bought some groceries,
> filled the car with gas, and mailed a letter before I came home.

This is not a story even though it includes a sequence of connected actions and covers a completed unit of time. The reader is tempted to say, "So what?"

This version is a little better:

> One morning before I drove downtown, I looked for Tabby, our cat, but couldn't find her. She was probably making her daily rounds of the neighborhood, so I left to do my errands. I bought groceries, filled the car with gas, and mailed a letter. After I parked the car in the garage, Tabby calmly crawled out from under the hood and strutted to the door to be let in.

A story must have a point, a reason for telling it. This story proves again that cats have nine lives.

> My grandmother celebrated her 100th birthday with a party of a hundred guests, a monstrous cake, and enough candles to start a conflagration.

This celebration in itself is not yet a story. When you tell me that she pioneered in western Kansas in the 1870s, raised a family by herself and put them all through school, then went back to school herself, you have a story.

Study this personal narrative by a freshman college student. It is not a professional piece, but it has a beginning, a middle, and an end. It also has some tension, or conflict, important to make a story interesting.

One evening, my homework piled up on my desk. To get away from it, I strolled to the men's lounge, where several guys were engaged in a fascinating card game nicknamed "Guts." It involved throwing pennies into a pot. The winner of each hand of cards won the pot. The mere sight of winning money triggered me to get involved in the game. While learning the game's basics, I lost money, but after I caught on, I slowly moved into the winning column. By the time we finished playing, I had won a dime.

I enjoyed the game thoroughly and returned the following evening. My luck turned and I lost 30 cents. To win back my money, I played a third evening. By now, I was addicted. When I won, I gambled my winnings. When I lost, I gambled to win it back.

I lost again the third evening. I joined the group another two evenings, becoming totally exhausted. I fell behind in my homework. All that mattered was making money. I wrapped myself tightly in the desire to make money. I lost all sense of the value of money. I treated it as nothing as I gambled it away foolishly.

After five evenings of gambling, I came to my senses. I realized I was abusing myself. Never before had anything tested my willpower to break the bond that greed had over me. I returned to my former standards and values. Breaking that bond took guts and willpower. Now as I look back over the ordeal, I have learned not only that money is

> something to respect, but that I should allow all my values,
> goals, and ideals to grow deep roots into common sense.

When you have finished telling your story, quit writing. Don't keep explaining and moralizing. Give the reader credit for some common sense.

This student wanted to tell the reader about his first gambling experience. He developed into a respected church leader and probably laughs at this intense experience with money as a college freshman.

WRITING TIP:

The secret of good storytelling is to move as close to the experience as possible. As you write, ask yourself what you heard, smelled, saw, felt at the time. Take the reader by the hand and lead him or her through the event. Work like a photographer with a zoom lens. Get so close to the experience that your reader feels the sun beating mercilessly down on you as you hoed potatoes or chopped cotton as a child, hears the crunch of snow under your boots in northern Minnesota, or nails popping in the siding in the bitterly cold winters of northern Saskatchewan. Make your reader shiver when you describe the harsh wail of the wind around the corners of a house on a homestead in Kansas.

WRITING OPTION:

A memoir writer helps readers experience and understand what he or she has gone through. How can you help the reader understand that prejudice hurts; that winning a prize, even a small one, brings joy; that being shoved aside brings disappointment? You can do this by selecting significant or telling facts, rather than a lot of opinionated words. Emotional reaction in the reader results when the significance of the facts becomes clear.

Choose an experience, a place, building, or person about which or whom you had strong feelings, negative or positive. Negative feelings usually work better when you do this the first time. I can recall having lunch at a greasy-spoon restaurant years ago in a small community. I was disgusted, even though the place had been recommended. What stimuli caused my disgust? How can I get the reader to feel this disgust? By selecting significant facts.

> *Sight: a fly crawling over the tablecloth; egg yolks*
>   *scabbed on the fork near my plate.*
> *Smell: rancid fat coming from the kitchen fryer.*
> *Taste: coffee with a bitter taste.*
> *Touch: sticky edges on the table.*
> *Hearing: a jukebox blaring loud music, a waitress*
>   *hollering my order to the cook a mile away.*

All the facts I selected create one central impression. Write a paragraph about a subject that will cause the reader to have the same reaction you had. Avoid adjectives and adverbs that express opinions. Let facts and verbs do the work. To be disgusted by something does not make the reader feel disgusted until you have shown, not told, why you felt that way.

In our family of seven, doing dishes after each meal was a major event, so we girls took turns by the week either washing, drying, or cleaning up. When it was my turn to dry, I worked at the task methodically, first drying forks, then spoons, then knives, and then going on to other objects in the same way. After I had done six of everything, I dried the tableware that remained, knowing that this time around there wouldn't be as many.

Dusting was another of my hated jobs, which included the stairs to the second floor and all sills and ledges. I wanted to learn to cook, but that specialized task was reserved for my older sisters, until one day I persuaded Mother to let me make some mayonnaise, the *pièce de résistance* of any chef. I followed the recipe carefully, yet my mayonnaise curdled, leaving ugly flecks of yellow yolk floating in a watery soup. I was sent back to dusting. Step one, swipe left to right; step two, swipe right to left; step three, swipe left to right, and on and on.

WRITING OPTION:

Write about a disappointment you experienced as a child. Why were you disappointed? My uncle, Abe Funk, told me this story before he died, not to show his disappointment but his mother's pain.

During the famine in the Ukraine in 1920, my brother and I, both young boys at the time, set out our plates one Christmas in the traditional manner with our names on them. We fully expected St. Nicholas to bring us Christmas goodies as usual. Before we went to bed, we left the door unlocked to let St. Nick into the house.

But times had changed. Hunger, disease, and starvation were rampant. Though the family pantry was empty, we young boys still hoped that in the morning our plates would be piled high as usual. Christmas morning we ran into the kitchen, happy to find two little newspaper–wrapped packages on each plate. As we unwrapped them, Mother watched, her eyes brimming with tears.

Although she was as hungry as everyone else in the family, she had deprived herself of a slice of bread, cut it into four pieces, and wrapped each one, in order to give each of us two. We boys sucked on those cubes of hard, dry bread for hours, never chewing it, to make it last longer. Many a time, I stood in the doorway to the pantry, looking at the empty shelves, remembering when they were filled with wonderful food.

The following is my most published story. In 1966, I was sitting in a Sunday school class in Kansas when the teacher, a retired missionary to China, told us about itinerating in northern Saskatchewan during the 1930s and hearing this account of events. After church I immediately wrote down all details I could remember and sent it off. My first editor waffled about publishing it because he didn't know whether it was true or folklore. You decide. Either way it makes a good story.

A Pig for a Pig

"I'll kill that man."

I nearly fell off the high seat of the Bennett wagon, where I was perched holding the reins of the horses. What had Dad said?

"I need land, Heinrichs, need it awful bad, or else I'll have to go out working as a farmhand again. I'll have a way of handling that man."

I tried to see Dad's face, but he was turned from me and I couldn't tell whether he was joking or not. My dad kill someone? Something was wrong. A ball of cold lead formed in my throat and settled heavily in my stomach. I wished we were at home.

The afternoon had been discouraging. Only last week, the notice had come in the mail that the farm we were sharecropping had been sold over our heads. We would have to move off before seedtime. But where to? There wasn't another farm available for miles. All afternoon, I had listened to Dad talking land to everyone he met. I had watched the worry lines coming out on his face as one man after another could give him no information. Tiredness had crept into his voice and his walk as we turned to the wagon to go home.

Old Mr. Heinrichs had met us there. He pushed his limp felt hat back on his head to scratch his thinning hair in response to Dad's familiar question.

"Can't say that I know of anything. Well now, come to think of it, the farm across from Jud Brewster's will likely be empty this spring. The renters on it now are planning to leave. No one stays on that farm long. It's rundown and next to impossible to live with Jud Brewster across the road. He drives everyone off."

"He wouldn't drive me off," Dad had replied quietly. His voice had sounded just a little cheerier.

"You don't know him. An angel couldn't live next to him, he's that mean."

Dad mumbled something and I caught only the last phrase, "I'll kill that man."

My brother Jimmie came rushing to meet me one day
the next week with the exciting words, "We're moving,
we're moving!" And the next week we moved.

Darkness had settled heavily over the unfamiliar
surroundings of the new farmyard when the last coop of
chickens was brought over. As we emptied them into the
henhouse, a few birds escaped the hatch and fluttered
noisily to the branches of the nearby poplars.

The folks were tired. Uncle Henry, who was helping
us, had already gone home. My bones ached and little
Jimmie was already stretched out on a mattress Mom had
placed on the kitchen floor. I dropped heavily beside him.
As I was drifting off, I dimly heard Dad and Mom praying
together by the kitchen table about being good neighbors
to Jud Brewster. You don't pray for men you intend to kill. I
must have misunderstood Dad the other day.

It seemed as if I had been sleeping only minutes when
a heavy-handed knock shattered the stillness. It was morning and light was seeping through the cracks in the old
green window shades. Dad jumped into his pants and was
at the door before I could even throw off my covers.

At the door stood our new neighbor, a big dark-haired
man in an ugly mood. Lying on my mattress, looking up
at him, I could only think of one thing – a picture of the
giant Goliath in our Bible storybook as he scowled down at

young David. David had been sure of victory. I felt absolutely helpless.

"Those roosters of yours in the trees next to the road have been bothering me all morning," he snarled. "You better make sure they don't bother me again, or I'll make sure they don't." He tapped the barrel of his rifle ominously.

With those words he stalked off, giving Dad no opportunity to apologize or even to explain. Dad turned to us boys. "Up, all of you, and get those chickens into the henhouse before you go to school. Now out, all of you."

For a long time, we heard nothing more from our new neighbor. We began to think the ugly rumors were only telephone gossip. Even timid Mrs. Brewster seemed almost pleased when Mom brought her a jar of new pincherry jelly she had made and invited her over for afternoon tea.

She never did come, for the next day trouble descended on us like Niagara Falls. Our cows got into Brewster's oats. The fences were bad all over. Dad saw them almost right away and rushed Mom and us boys over to drive them out, but Mr. Brewster was there before us. He swore and cursed and raved at us, waving his old pitchfork around in wild gestures. Dad shooed us boys away, but even from behind the poplar clump where we hid, we could hear him calling Dad down. We edged around the bushes to watch and when I saw Dad paying old Jud some money, one bill after another, I knew then and there I would be walking to school again this fall. My new bicycle was walking off in his dirty pocket. I hated Jud Brewster.

There were lots of little things after that which brought Jud Brewster storming to our farm, carrying his gun, such as our dog chasing his chickens, or we boys pulling down his haymow, when we wouldn't even go near his place.

One hot afternoon Dad was in the barn sharpening his ax at the emery wheel and we boys were fooling around behind the barn, when we heard Jud Brewster bark out, "Janzen, your pigs have been into my garden and rooted up all my vegetables. I've warned you!" The word were pouring out. "You know what that means, Janzen!"

We boys crept around the barn so that we could hear a little better.

"You've made too many promises, Janzen," he roared, "and now I've brought you your pigs back. They'll never get into my garden again."

Dad came out of the barn and we all turned to follow Mr. Brewster's arm movement as he pointed to the wagon a short distance away. It was loaded with our complete herd of young pigs – but each one was dead, shot by the rifle of our angry neighbor. The silence became almost heavy. Time stopped. Blood plopped slowly into the soft dust of the driveway from the cracks in the wagon. A bird chirping in the treetop seemed to sound from another world.

The ax Dad was grinding slipped from his hands and time moved ahead again. Dad's face glistened with perspiration as he said quietly, "Come, boys, let's get rid of the pigs." He never spoke to our neighbor.

About a month later, just before chore time, little Jimmie came rushing in, shrieking at the top of his voice. "Daddy, go get a gun quick. Jud Brewster's pigs are in our garden."

"We can get a gun from the Thompsons," I piped up, tearing to the door. The taste of vengeance was already sweet in my mouth. Dad didn't believe in owning a gun, but I knew the Thompsons always had one.

"Hold on, boys, we won't need a gun." Dad put a restraining hand on my shoulder. "You harness up the lumber wagon and we'll return those pigs before we do the chores tonight."

It took a lot of chasing and hard work before we had that miserable herd of pigs up the ramp. It would have been easier to load them dead, but Dad had explained that this was the Bible way of doing it. With Dad guiding the reins of the horses, we marched down the road to our neighbor's house. Dad and we younger boys stepped up to the back door while Henry drove around the pigpen.

"Good evening, Mr. Brewster. Your pigs were into my garden and I've brought them back."

Jud Brewster staggered back, his face white with fear, his hands clawing the air aimlessly. "My pigs," he croaked, "my pigs … in your garden." He reeled against the door frame for support.

"Yes, we've brought them back. They're in the wagon over there. Where shall we put them?"

Mr. Brewster didn't even turn to look. His face became even more ashen. His body sagged against the door. "Just dump them over behind the barn."

"But if I put them there, they'll just get out again. Let's get them into the pigpen and make sure the fence is fixed so that they can't get out again."

Hope sprang into the frightened man's eyes. "You mean you brought them back alive? They're not dead?"

"Why, yes, I have them in the wagon."

Our neighbor clutched Dad's hands and he wept. "You didn't kill them? Man, how can you act like this to me after what I've done to you?"

That ended the excitement for us. Dad and Mr. Brewster talked for such a long time that we had to go home and do the chores alone. When he finally came home, he brought half of Mr. Brewster's pigs with him. The next Sunday, the Brewsters came to church with us and stayed for Sunday dinner. He wasn't such a bad guy after all when he got changed around inside.

It wasn't until the next spring when I was pumping up the tire of my new bicycle that I remembered to ask Dad about what he had said to Mr. Heinrichs about killing Jud Brewster.

"Not with a gun, or anything like that, son," Dad replied. "I planned to do it another way, like the Bible says, by heaping coals of fire on his head. It took a long time to get those coals hot enough, but it worked. That old neighbor is as dead as a doornail, just like I said he would be."

BECOMING
COMFORTABLE WITH
YOUR FAMILY'S STORY

I t is easy to get hooked on "roots mania." With me it started with a little notation in a family genealogy about a relative, long ago, being a witch in the Ukraine. It took me years to figure that one out. Mother couldn't quite explain it. Dad couldn't explain it, either, although the woman was his cousin. Decades later, in Kansas, I met another relative who had known the mysterious "witch" well. Flaunting traditional church and community traditions, she smoked and wore colorful skirts and shawls and earned her living telling fortunes with Tarot cards. She was called *Haaxrampelsche*, a derisive term. But she was family.

We all have connections to a family. To get started in recording your personal or family history, become a hoarder. Guard zealously anything you can find related to family history such as documents, letters, diaries, photographs, scraps of stories, home movies, military records, tax records, ledgers, census records, and memories. To write easily and well, it is important to become comfortable with your family's story and understand who they were. That gives you a head-start on writing your own story.

Use the Internet often. Google names frequently. It may surprise you what you will find. You can locate most obituaries in the United States on the Internet. Once you have an obituary, you can often make a four- or five-generation tree from the information it provides. Sometimes it also gives information about where the family lived and what they did.

Set up a filing system to give order to your material. Use a box if you haven't got a filing cabinet. Write down where you found a fact or story immediately. I file generally first by family lines (father's, mother's, then brother and sisters, children, specific subjects, and so forth). I know my way around my filing system, but not everyone else might.

Which brings me to my next point: Your family history has many details and stories, but usually one central theme. In working with your material over time, you will discover that theme. As you keep working with your family history, you will see patterns emerging of thinking, speaking, and doing. Sometimes this awareness comes slowly, but don't get impatient. It will dawn on you eventually what made your family tick.

The Glass Castle is Jeanette Walls' story about her unique childhood, living in a home where her parents refused to conform to society's ideas of responsibility. The theme is soon clear. Her father was an alcoholic and her mother had grandiose ideas about her creativity. Her parents left their children to fend for themselves for even the most basic of needs, such as food and shelter. What came through to me was the author's courage and strength in the face of odds, untouched by anger or self-pity.

In one of my own memoirs, I wrote about the relationships between parents and children.

> I recall my mother, like many mothers at the time, telling us children to be sure to always wear clean underwear in case of an accident. Our life blood might be gushing to the pavement, but we could die peacefully because our underwear was clean. We had not shamed the family.
>
> This little incident says something about my family and similar families. What is it? It was important not to bring disgrace to the family when you lived in a small close-knit community. Today, what EMT cares about your underwear? But the emphasis on "what will the people think?" was an early theme in our family along with honesty, punctuality, and cleanliness – almost above godliness. We were a well-ordered family. Our daily life together had structure and purpose. We were always expected to be aware that we had neighbors who saw our every move.

If you made a family tree earlier, by now you should have a fairly complete list of names of close relatives and their relationship to you. This is the first step in getting comfortable with your family's story.

Focus first on your grandparents. What was their place of origin? Where did they grow up? What brought them together? What was their livelihood?

How well did you know your grandparents? You want facts, but you also want information on the quality of relationships and the type of life they lived. Become familiar with your grandparents' story. As I wrote about my own family:

> I only had one grandparent I was aware of, so grandparenting was not a familiar concept to me as a child. The other grandparents had been left behind in Russia. One died of typhus during the Russian Revolution of 1917–19 before I was born. My maternal grandmother died of an unidentified disease and malnutrition in the famine that followed. I cherish a long letter from my grandfather describing her death that I discovered in my adulthood. He also died of an unidentified illness and malnutrition a few years later during the Stalinist years. Medical attention was unheard of. In that letter to my parents in faraway Canada, he became a real person with concerns and sensitivities.

Focus next on your parents. Who were they? What was your mother's maiden name? Interview them if they are still alive. If not, interview siblings to find out details of their lives. Where did they live? What did they do for a living?

My father's younger brother, Peter J. Funk, wrote a short auto-biography before he died. As you read the following excerpt, which details can I assume also applied to my father, who grew up in the same home, only a few years ahead of Uncle Peter?

Life was simple in my childhood home in the Ukraine. Everything was homemade or could be made by someone in the village. The rest was bought from peddlers who dropped by. My brother Nick broke a window one summer, and it couldn't be replaced until fall when the peddler who sold window panes came around. One peddler sold pots and pans, and one old lady sold small items such as needles and thread.

My brother Henry made us our *Schlorren*, wooden-soled sandals, out of willow trees. Sometimes younger children inherited an older sibling's footwear. Since wood will not bend, walking was difficult. To make that easier Henry nailed a piece of leather over a cut in the wood under the ball of the foot. A piece of leather over the toes held the footwear in place. From early spring until late fall we went barefoot.

During the summer, bathing was no problem because we boys spent a lot of time in the Dnieper River. Winter bathing was a different story. About once a month, usually on a Saturday afternoon, Mother would say, "Bath time!" Everyone bathed in a tub somebody had made, just big enough to sit in.

First, we had to carry water into the house from the well. Next, start a fire in the hearth and heat the water in pots or pans. When the water was hot, Henry, being the oldest, got in first. Mother poured water over him and he lathered himself with her homemade soap, strong enough to take the spots off a leopard. Next, it was Nick's turn. By the time it was my turn, you could almost walk on the water.

Mother had three cures: a spoonful of honey for a sore throat, and a spoonful of some brown syrup called *Alpenkraeuter* for almost everything. Her third remedy was "go sit in the backhouse till you feel better." I spent a lot of time in that little house meditating. There was no use complaining to her. She just sent me back out again. Anyway it cured a lot of ailments. I guess her theory was if that if you survive, the illness was not fatal.

Find the origin of your family name. Get all the possible spellings of your name. Sometimes this is possible on the Internet. What is its meaning? What changes did it go through over the decades?

Ruth Kanin in *Write the Story of Your Life* states that Paul Revere's name was originally DeRivoire, then Rivoire. Later, his father changed it to Revere so that "the bumpkins could pronounce it." Boston city records have spelled it as Reviere, Reveiere, Revear, and Reverie. One woman found an ancestor with the letters MD following his name. She was overjoyed to have found a doctor. However, at the time (1760), MD stood for "mule driver." The lesson? Do your research before making assumptions.

What were your parents' circumstances at the time they got married? Do you know anything about their courtship? What brought them together? Was this a love relationship or an arranged marriage? My mother told me she married my father because of his spiritual outlook on life. A serious thinker herself, she wanted this in the man she committed herself to.

What was the education and occupation of each parent? Was your mother a full-time homemaker or did she work outside the home? Was she a good housekeeper or homemaker? Was your father a good provider? Was money an issue in your childhood home? Did sons follow their fathers into the same occupation? What was the prevailing attitude toward women working outside the home?

Why did they set up housekeeping where they did? Did they live with parents or other people? What social class did each come from? Were they racially the same? Did it matter? Was anyone in the family ever labeled a "black sheep?"

What activities or values were important to each parent? What did they disagree about? Did they have strong religious faith and practices? How was this evidenced in daily life? What were their regular religious practices? What was their state of health generally?

My husband and I and our children moved several times during our 15 years of marriage. We started out life in Yarrow, British Columbia, but that job dried up. Back we went to Saskatchewan for several years, then on to Manitoba to pursue my husband's dream of religious journalism. After graduation we moved back to Saskatchewan to teaching and a pastorate, but the dream persisted, so we moved to Ontario when I was seven months pregnant with my youngest child. I was not a happy camper, but in those days, wives and families moved with the husband.

Compare my experience, which we decided as a couple, with that of my mother's, when about 20,000 Mennonites left South Russia for Canada during the 1920s. In the following excerpt from her biography, my mother explains why she and my father and two toddlers migrated to Canada. The year was 1923, two years after the Russian Revolution had subsided, but those years had been full of illness, poverty, hardship, and lawlessness. The Mennonite colonies in southern Ukraine had been left in economic, cultural, social, and religious ruin. Mother speaks:

> Talk about migration erupted in our village of Rosental and never died down. Debates about whether to leave or to stay were long, loud, and sometimes angry.
>
> "Times will improve. They can never get as bad as they were."
>
> "People in Canada don't want us, for they fear we will take away their jobs. They are planning to protest before the government for giving us *Russlaender* visas."
>
> My brothers said that if they had enjoyed the good times, they should be able to endure a few bad years. My father was afraid to cross the ocean. He was also afraid of the Indians about which he had read.
>
> Migration fever intensified in our small village the day that my husband Jake's brother John came home with the report that the military had lopped off the head of his close friend, known for criticizing the new Bolshevik regime. They had spiked it on a pole and paraded it down the

street as a warning to anyone considering resisting the new government. John applied for exit visas for himself and his family the next day.

Jake was still too close to conscription age to feel comfortable in Russia. His 4½ years in the army as an orderly would count for nothing if another war broke out. Furthermore, his prospects of ever owning land were slim. If we left, we had lost nothing and could hope for everything in the new country of Canada. He hesitated, though not for long. His mother and I pressured him to start working on our exit papers. If he didn't do it, we would. He went to work. We left Rosental on July 2, 1923.

– Anna Janzen Funk, in *Anna Janzen Funk's Story: Childhood to Coming to Canada* as told to the author over a period of years.

Did you inherit any of your parents' letters, diaries, and so forth? What was the driving force of each parent? Was it to achieve in life? To get all the children well educated and established in life? To bring justice to others? If you were writing an obituary for each parent, what outstanding characteristic would you want readers to remember about each one? As I wrote about my mother:

My mother put hospitality above all else. A guest was always welcomed warmly and offered a cup of tea, and possibly an array of pastries. "Here, have some; they're good." She had been a cook in a large mental institution in the Ukraine for five years as a young woman and knew her skills. She often stood at her open door waiting for me when I came. When I left she kept waving until I was well out of sight. My father, on the other hand, was concerned with bringing fairness to others, having suffered indignities and been ostracized as a young boy for being left-handed, hurts from which he suffered a lifetime.

WRITING OPTION:

Write about the relationship of your parents (birth or adoptive) as you remember it. Was it an intimate relationship or distant? What story best illustrates the relationship of your parents to one another? Was it related to money, to discipline, to religion, or politics? Or perhaps something else? Were they romantically inclined toward one another?

WRITING OPTION:

Write about a move your family made, or a time your father or mother changed work or profession, and how it affected you. Or write about what it meant to your family to stay in one community a long time. Compare and contrast what changed and what stayed the same and the effects.

ONE LIFE,
MANY STAGES

Stories are a way of keeping the memory of a deceased person alive, Tim O'Brien wrote in his Vietnam War novel *The Things They Carried.* I think of these stories as lengthening a person's shadows, extending their influence beyond his or her natural life. One of your goals is to lengthen the shadows of your own life so that they extend into the lives of children and grandchildren, giving them a sense of your values and commitments.

In this chapter, I will discuss writing about the developmental stages we move through on our way to maturity. It is important to identify and become familiar with the full sweep of your personal story so you can retrieve all parts on demand.

Stage 1: Connecting With the Early Years

Novelist John Updike wrote, "Memories, impressions, and emotions from your first 20 years on Earth are most writers' main material; little that comes afterward is quite so rich and resonant." His words hold true for memoir writers. What general feelings do you have about your early childhood? Happiness? Misery? Bliss? What contributed to that feeling? Was it a combination of low conflict, low economic stress, a general sense of moral order and the importance of getting along with others, along with a strong religious emphasis? Or was it a combination of negative factors such as dissent, alcoholism, indifference, and illness?

Think again about one of the houses where you spent many years. What did the house look like? Was it kept spiffed up and painted or do you remember it as run down? Did it have an inside bathroom or a little house with a path? Did your mother keep a garden? What about the inside? What kind of furniture did your family own? Which objects did your mother treasure in particular? What stories come to mind in connection with the various rooms, pieces of furniture, yard, and garage?

My oldest daughter, Joanna Wiebe Baer, wrote about her childhood memories in a letter to me:

> I think you made such a great nest for us. ... I remember sitting on the sofa reading *Blue Willow* in my new gray sweater with the rhinestones, which I really loved. The

wooden wall phone was a scary and a mysterious object.
We had two record players, one for us kids. I liked the set
of classical records you got then and also the kid records.
You always kept the house very clean, and as a child I
appreciated the order, neatness, and shiny clean surfaces.
I remember the door to Daddy's study, the piano, your
writing desk under the stairs by the window, which looked
out in the direction of the slough – north, I think.

The kitchen is especially clear. The low counters, the
sink with the green pump, the dark woodstove, the kitchen
table, which I helped to set for dinner. I remember you
teaching me how to gather lettuce and dress it with vinegar
and sugar – one of my favorite dishes.

I remember the cellar with its heaps of potatoes, looking
for good ones. Hanging my coat by the door on the porch.
The stairs to the second floor. The time the kittens had your
dresser drawer as their first home – to your dismay.

I was so happy in my own room, which had a single
window facing south. I picked prairie violets and put
them in a little glass jar on the table. In bed, I would read
the Bible, all of it sounding very important and virtually
unintelligible to me. I looked at every page, read much of
it. I would pull the covers up to my nostrils and warm up,
breathing the cool room air. The other bedroom remains
cloudy. The bathroom was a place to get in and out of fast.
I would rather go outside, even in cold weather.

The house was a place of safety. I loved to roam all day outside, to play with other children or to be by myself. But then how wonderful to come home to sit down to potatoes and cracklings, the world's most comforting dish, or fresh–baked soft bread with *Gruebenschmaltz* on it. Or chicken soup, or kohl rabi. Always something wonderful to eat.

My final memory is of polishing the floors with rags tied to my shoes, listening to the radio, opera, I think, on Saturday afternoon, with lovely smells of floor wax, bread and furniture polish and the prairie breeze all mixed together, the sunlight slanting through the windows and gleaming on the floor. I was content. The house was my home. I felt at home there.

Notice that she went from room to room, describing fixtures and activities as they related to her as a child. What she doesn't mention is the time she found a dead bird, wrapped it in cloth, and placed it carefully in the space next to her room. The smell finally made her retrieve it and give it a better resting place.

Try doing the same as she did, going from room to room, recovering memories. Here's one of my childhood memories.

I felt secure and happy in my childhood home, even though it was very modest with no modern conveniences. We had a playhouse attached to the garage, so many good memories are associated with that little room, as well as the garden, outhouse, and steam bath (sauna) plunked near the back alley. I have lots of stories about the outhouse and sauna, some of which are found in my book, *Good Times with Old Times*. As a child, I assumed all children had playhouses. I found out later we were privileged children in this respect.

When Mother and Dad arrived in Saskatoon, Saskatchewan, in 1923 from the Ukraine, with little more than what they had on their backs, they were hosted in the home of a relative. Their hostess showed them around the house and yard. In the back yard was a small playhouse for the children with clean, starched curtains on the windows. Unbelievable! Mother never forgot that. In the Soviet Union, having survived World War I and the Russian Revolution, and then the famine and typhus epidemic that followed, curtains for the house were an unknown luxury. Playhouses did not exist in the old country. All spare wood was burned to stay warm. I have since wondered whether that little playhouse was the reason Mother gave us girls curtains to hang on its window.

Was yours a blended family or a single-parent family? In some traditions, it was common to take in orphaned children of relatives or friends. What was the climate in the home at the time of the blending or when you became a one-parent family because of death, divorce, or separation? Who visited you during your childhood years? Were family reunions common? What about neighbors? What was your family's relationship to neighbors?

Who were your neighbors? Were there any empty lots you played in? Did your parents consider your neighborhood a safe place for children? As a child, did you experience violence of any kind, including theft or burglary, domestic and child abuse?

When you were a child, did someone persuade you to do something despicable or demeaning, such as torture an animal or make fun of a handicapped person? Or did someone persuade you to move beyond yourself to do something good and worthwhile?

> When I was in high school a friend asked me to bicycle to the lake about 25 miles away with her boyfriend and her. I found out later her mother wouldn't have let her go without someone along to "chaperone" her. My being present didn't seem to matter to the lovey–dovey twosome. I felt used at the end of the day because I was not part of their conversation and activities.

Childhood is often a time of fear and terror of dark places under the bed, in the cellar, or the hidden recesses of the barn. Did you have such fears? How did you overcome them? When did you learn that someday you will die, but that dying is all right because it is part of life? Was it when a pet died or you saw your first dead person?

How big was your world when you were a child? When did you first become aware that the world reached far beyond the limits of your farmyard, village, or even state?

When did your "baby" name change to something more adult? When did Jimmie or Sonny become James, and Peggy become Margaret? Was that your choice? Did you ever have a nickname? Did you like it?

Can you remember receiving an item of new clothing? Where did the family money come from? How was money given to the church or charities? My parents believed in giving to the church. In addition to what they gave, before we walked into church each Sunday morning, Dad pressed a nickel into five little hands to put in the Sunday school offering. Sometimes what he and we put in together was more than the rest of the entire congregation, mostly farmers who didn't have an income during the Depression years. Dad also believed in giving to the poor because he had known the pangs of hunger and the dearth of needed possessions, such as shoes, when he was a young man.

One fall during the Depression, my mother made me a coat out of her old black coat with a shiny fur collar. I refused to wear it, and, instead, wore my thin short skating jacket all winter in the bitterly cold weather of northern Saskatchewan. I was not about to wear "an old woman's coat." I was defending my dignity. Mother was concerned that I stay warm despite our family's lack of money. I don't remember what I wore the next few years, but in my last

> year of high school, my father bought me a long winter
> coat in a beautiful shade of turquoise with astrakhan fur,
> probably fake, trimming the collar and down the front. I
> felt like a princess

As a child, were you ever aware of the social class you belonged to? Did you feel discriminated against because of who you were, what you wore, and where your family lived, or did your family assume they were as good if not better than anyone else?

What is your ethnic origin? How important is it to you now? What are some traditions your family practiced when you were a child? Describe some ethnic foods your family ate. Is your religious denomination associated with an ethnic group? Who are some important people who belong to your ethnic group or denomination?

What was the prevailing attitude toward teachers in your childhood? Who were your teachers?

What values and habits did your parents instill in you as a child, such as hard work, honesty, punctuality, thrift, and cleanliness? You usually will find a story around each of these qualities. One writing class member shared a sad story about his first pair of new shoes.

> The family was poor, but his parents managed to scrape
> together enough money to buy him a pair of shoes to start
> school in fall during the Depression. Little Johnny was
> strictly admonished not to wear the shoes until the first
> day of school, but temptation was too strong. He sneaked

out wearing them to the pond nearby. To his horror, he got stuck in the soft soil on the shore, and, as he lifted his feet, his other shoe fell off and floated away with the stream. He reluctantly limped home with one shoe to tell his mother the sad tale. She told him they had no money to buy another pair.

When school started he had to wear his brother's old too-big shoes, with cardboard insoles to cover the holes. The first day of school went well, but he forgot some of the hundreds of new rules such as going to the bathroom during recess. Play was more important. After recess, the pressure inside built up by the minute, so he raised his hand with one finger pointed up in the traditional code of all schools to let the teacher know his urgent need.

"It's almost noon, Johnny," said his teacher. "You can wait."

When she called him to the board to see if he could write his name, he picked up the chalk to start the first letter, but nature was stronger. Warm liquid gushed down his legs into his brother's old shoes. He dashed out of the classroom, feet squishing in his too-big shoes, home to mother, to tell her his new tale of woe.

His mother helped him change into a dry pair of pants and after lunch sent him back to school with a note. But Johnny couldn't face the teacher just yet, and he didn't know what his mother had written because he couldn't read, so he wrapped the note around a rock and threw it in an open window. All afternoon he wandered around the little village.

The next day he was back in his seat. Thereafter, if he as much as wiggled a little finger, let alone raised a hand with a finger reaching high, the teacher promptly said, "Johnny, you may leave the room."

That was an embarrassing childhood experience for Johnny, who later in life became a prominent educator. And who hasn't had a similar experience? Despite these minor mistakes, which looked huge back then, being a child can be wonderful. Do you remember looking at your little world of sandboxes, mud pies, sandlot baseball, or hanging over the corral fence to watch the wild horses being broken with a sense of wonder, even when your Christmas gift was only a tiny blue bottle of Evening in Paris *eau de cologne* that lost its scent with one dab?

WRITING OPTION:

Write about an incident as it relates to money and the way it was earned, spent, squandered, saved, given away, or handled in your home. This could be a long account or just one story. Were your parents rich or poor? Who earned the money? Who spent it? Who paid the bills? Were bills always paid on time? Did you get an allowance as a child? What did you spend it on? Do you remember your parents discussing money? What was the tone of their voices?

Did your mother work outside the home? If not, what did she do to
get pocket money for herself? Was gambling an issue in your home?
What about frugality, even stinginess?

Stage 2: Tracing Defining
Moments in Adolescence

In your adolescent years, from about age 13 to your late teens, what
was going on? Adolescence is a modern life stage. At one time, children
moved from childhood to young adulthood with no buffer zone to take
off the edge. Children were pushed into the work world sometimes as
young as 13 or 14. Girls married at 15 or 16. As you write about this
period, you want your readers to grasp what it was like when you were
this age, which sometimes was an awkward, uncomfortable, unsure
time. Don't be afraid to poke fun at yourself. That period is now over.
Give yourself freedom to look at yourself as a gawky, inept teenager.

Where were you living? How many siblings did you have? For
each of the items in the following list, mark whether you felt confident, upbeat about this aspect of your life, or frustrated, discouraged,
uncomfortable. Were you having a hilarious, confident or troubled,
desperate adolescence? Maybe you were indifferent. When you have
decided your feeling, ask yourself the reasons for it. Which adjectives
cause you to remember a story of some kind? Talk to your siblings
about this time. Your conversation will trigger many memories.

Aspects of adolescent life	Positive feelings	Negative feelings	Neutral
High school academics			
Dating experiences			
Clothing, hairstyles, fads			
Language			
Music, art, drama			
Movies, television, radio			
Athletics			
Student leadership			
Movies, radio, concerts			
Teachers, coaches, pastors			
Heroes, role models, celebrities			
Graduation, awards			
Religious stirrings and beliefs			
Church life			
Body image			
Sexual awareness and experiences			
Leaving home for the first time			
First work experiences			
Biggest trouble you ever got into			
Experiences with money			
Historic events of that era			
Friends and enemies			
Automobile use			
Substance abuse			

Was adolescence a time of turmoil or mostly smooth sailing? Did you have special friendships and love affairs that were important? Go ahead — write about them. It doesn't matter now. What banners did you wave fearlessly or timidly during your high school days? Adolescence is often the time when we felt inept because we didn't quite fit in. I remember when I thought I was part of the team that was going to compete in some athletic contest, and got dressed in shorts and a shirt and stood around with the important athletes only to find my name wasn't on the list. My heart plummeted into my shoes. I slunk to the sidelines to blend in with the spectators. Maybe you remember something similar.

One of my college students wrote this to describe a miserable high school experience:

It was simply a common practice in our high school, something everyone naturally did. But because I was the way I was, I couldn't join them, no matter how badly I wanted to. After the noon meal in the lunchroom, kids gathered in the study hall in separate groups of friends. It seemed to me as if each group, or clique, was competing with the others to see who could be the most boisterous or appear to be having the most fun.

When I entered seventh grade, I no longer had the security of only 30 classmates. Instead, I found myself among those awe-inspiring high schoolers. I was shy and lacking in self-confidence, especially around older, more sophisticated kids. My more aggressive friends quickly adopted the noon custom of joining study hall cliques. I drew back.

My skin broke out, leaving me feeling self-conscious, especially around boys. When someone unintentionally didn't answer my questions or return my smile, I was sure they were ignoring me. I dreaded being snubbed again as I had been in the third and fourth grades. Soon the easiest way out was to avoid study hall completely.

For a while, my friends kept inviting me, but I repeat-edly refused, so we parted ways after lunch. I was ashamed to walk aimlessly around the halls as if I didn't have any friends, so I either hid in the girls' restroom or pretended to go on an errand downtown. I was lonely, but too proud to admit it. I never told anyone about my lonely noon hours, so I suffered alone for two years because I had no crowd to fit into. I can identify with Charlie Brown. I believe God is helping me to gradually overcome my fears.

WRITING OPTION:

Think of one critical decision you made during your teen-age years, even if it's only small. Did you decide to wear something the others weren't wearing? When did you first forgive someone for a wrong against you? Did you decide to leave a party early? You can write an entire life story by tracing critical decisions or pivotal events in your life.

Stage 3: Finding the Markers
in Young Adulthood

When you divided your life into eight divisions (see Chapter 2), the first three were probably early childhood, grade school, and high school. The next stage probably covers one or more of the following: education, work or military, voluntary service, marriage.

In his book *Markings*, renowned diplomat Dag Hammarskjöld refers to the markings, or signposts, in his life by which he could trace his life's journey. Identifying your own markers enables you to retrace the pathway of your life, especially your inner journey, which is important, for it governed your outer life. All people have to work at life, or developmental, tasks in the maturing process.

We want to figure out the markings or signposts in our early adulthood. What age range does this period cover? That's debatable. I've heard experts talk about anything from post-high school to age 30 and even beyond that.

Young adults today aren't clear when they attain full adulthood. Is it when they turn 21, get married, have children, finish going to school, or fully support themselves? When did you truly feel like an adult? What did that feel like? A friend told me she knew she was an adult when there was no one else around to pick up the pieces. "Self-authority is a sign of adult thinking," writes Ruth Kanin in *Write the Story of Your Life*. During this stage, we usually begin to feel a small sense of mastery in some area.

In young adulthood, we usually become more aware of what is happening in the world beyond ourselves as it begins to move into our own lives. As you plan to write about this period, study the social and political history of the broader world during your young adult years. If you have strong connections to the church, study the history, not only of your denomination, but of what was happening in the broader religious community.

Psychologists say you only successfully learn the lessons of one life stage if you have successfully mastered earlier life stages. You learn intimacy with friends, for example, by first learning to trust your parents or other adults as a child or adolescent. You learn intimacy in marriage by first learning to trust friends in your teen years. Which of these changes in your young adulthood were unexpected: divorce of parents or siblings, your own early divorce, remaining single, immediate success or failure at a career, losing or finding personal faith, having a child before marriage? What lessons did you learn? The young adult years are usually crucial in determining the direction of life.

Work your way through the following questions, making notes as you go. However, don't be too quick to assign major "signpost" status to some life changes that were only geographical changes. Going to college may not have been as significant a turning point as something you learned or someone you met there (a teacher, friend, or spouse). Getting married may not have been as important as what you learned about intimacy. Having children may not have been as significant as what you learned about forgiveness and love.

1. At what age did you show initiative with regard to your own education? Who decided where you would go to college after high

school and why? Who supported you? If you didn't go to college, what happened instead?

Where did you attend and why? What was your major and why did you choose it? Were you an excellent, good, or mediocre student? How common was it for young people to go to college then? Was there much political activity on campus? What were your political views? How involved were you in drug or alcohol use on campus? Can you recall any influential teachers or friends? What was religious life like on campus?

2.   If you went into the military, why did you go? Conscription or self-enlistment? If you were a conscientious objector, what led you to this decision? What other attitudes toward war and the military were you aware of at the time? Did you consider taking a different approach? Were you a "my country right or wrong" kind of person, or did you think independently? What was the attitude of your family toward your decision? What do you remember about military training? About alternative service? What was the attitude toward women in the service?

3.   What are the "markings" or stages in your working life? Was it hard to go to work after school and Saturdays during high school? After high school? What kinds of jobs did you take during the summer? Did they influence your choice of a college major? Was working for money an important marker in your life? What factors or events led to your lifelong attitude toward money and wealth?

4.   What are the markings in your development of relationships with the opposite sex? As you think back to this time in your life, what was the prevailing attitude about courtship, marriage and family? Was it over-romanticized? Not realistic enough? How did people react to a couple living together? Do you remember a peer having a baby out of wedlock? How was she treated by the community?

Recall your first infatuation. How did it affect your actions, thoughts, and dreams? Did you doodle his or her name? Buy her a gift? Send him a note? Make a deliberate attempt to bump into her? Did the object of your affection know about this infatuation? How long did it last? Did it result in any kind of relationship? What are your feelings about this now?

As I look over the landscape of discarded boyfriends, I recall a young man smitten with my golden-haired beauty when I was 16. He saw me wearing a blue velvet beanie with a huge feather waving jubilantly. I didn't know what to do with him. He was insistent. I didn't like him. I didn't want him. He finally gave up. Another young man also fell in love and sent me a huge present from England, where he was stationed during the war. I thought he was interested in my sister, but Anne wasn't around. But then, I wasn't either. My father made me send it back. To England? Yes.

Did I ever fall in love also? Oh yes, with first one, then another, and another. My world lit up when Mike walked by our gate whistling "Mexicali Rose." He gave me a mother-of-pearl brooch with Kathleen on it in gold wiring. I assume it was intended for another girlfriend originally named Kathleen, but I still have it. Another boyfriend was taken over by my best girlfriend when I went on vacation. He never came back. A summer romance with a boogie-woogie piano player ended when he returned to a former girlfriend. Do I regret these infatuations? Not at all. They taught me something about men and relationships.

5. What are the stages in the development of your relationships within the family? When did you and your siblings become friends? How did you feel about leaving home the first time? Was this an easy passage? Did you ever move back home, even for a short time?

I returned home for six weeks after my first daughter was born because we had no place to live while my husband went to summer school. Living at home with Mother and Dad felt so good, and they loved baby Joanna. Though I was now a mother, supposedly an adult, it felt good to be mothered.

6. Can you think of times you were challenged to change your attitude from self-pity to self-esteem? "Self-esteem" was an unknown term when I was a child. We were often admonished not to be proud of our accomplishments because pride was the sin by

which the angel Lucifer fell. What about humility and arrogance? Honesty and dishonesty? Love and forgiveness? Generosity and stinginess? Punctuality and procrastination? Affirmation and criticism?

7. What new skills did you learn after high school? I recall college freshmen who had to learn to do laundry, manage money, even open a can of soup and heat it. When did you learn these skills, or to balance a bank book?

8. During these young adult years, what gave you joy? What made you feel unhappy?

9. What was the first means of transportation you owned? A bicycle? A car? What is the farthest you traveled from home with or without your family? At what age did you learn to drive?

10. Did you have heroes or role models among teachers, religious leaders, relatives, celebrities, fictional characters? What about life goals? Were they clear or fuzzy? How did the life goals of men and women in your early adulthood differ from today?

11. What was the role of alcohol, tobacco, and illegal drugs in your life as a young adult? Did you ever have any encounters with the law for any reason?

12. Did you ever feel discriminated against because of gender or race as a young adult? What happened?

13. Describe your first year of marriage if it took place during this period. What adjectives best describe it? Any particular problems in adjusting to marriage? Try to be honest about this. Was your marriage mostly a following of tradition and the wild movement of hormones? Did you know your spouse as well as you thought you did? What did you argue about? What are the good memories of these first years of marriage? How did you relate to your in-laws?

Young adulthood is such an important period to write about, it requires much careful thought. Before you move on to the next period, review this entire period.

1. What were the highlights of your young adult years?

2. What were the down times of this period?

3. Did you like yourself during this time? Why or why not? What was a wished-for accomplishment during this period, such as a few more friends, to lose weight, a deeper inner life, better relationships with parents, better earning capacity, or more education?

4. What were young people's attitudes toward sex when you were growing up? Many people say that one of the biggest changes in

the modern world is in attitudes toward sex — the so-called sexual revolution.

5.   Do you recall any particular conflicts with members of an older generation?

Some last thoughts about this period. Annie Dillard writes in her memoir *An American Childhood*: "I leave out many things that were important to my life but of no concern for the present book, like the summer I spent in Wyoming when I was 15. I keep the action in Pittsburgh; I see no reason to drag everybody off to Wyoming just because I want to tell them about my summer vacation." She adds that a memoir writer should not hang onto the reader's arm, like a drunk, and say, "And then I did this and it was so interesting." She also leaves out her private involvement with various young men. She leaves out anything that might trouble her family. She is not tempted to air grievances.

WRITING OPTION:

Pick one turning point or critical decision that stands out during your young adulthood and explore it more fully. What normal transitions or changes did you expect to move through, such as getting an education, getting a job, getting married and learning to live with your spouse, having children (or not), making friends, and developing a world view. Which of these didn't happen?

Think back to the atmosphere of that period; perhaps it was the turbulent 1960s. Write down as quickly as possible adjectives or metaphors that come to mind as you think through that period. What kind of person were you then? What kind of person were you becoming? What was your attitude toward life, your goals, religious beliefs or commitments to any group or teaching? What resources were available to you at the time of decision-making? Start the assignment by saying, "The 1960s were a time when I ...."

Describe the turning point without judgment. Some decisions may seem like wrong ones now. Simply write down what happened. You want to be authentic. Too much of our past is often glossed over to make it look better to ourselves and to others.

Stage 4: A Look at the Middle Years (not middle age)

As we have seen, young adulthood is often the time life makes a turn from one kind of life to another – forward or backwards. These moments may not always be productive or pleasant, but we have to deal with them. In working with the middle years, you want to identify the markings, or turning points, that continue to happen. My husband's death, for example, was a major unexpected turning point at age 38. It meant I had to return to work to support my family. Eventually, it led to my returning to school to be able to teach and to a long chain of further events.

When are you an honest-to-goodness middle adult? Once again, chronological age is not always the determining factor. The middle years differ for each person. In our society with a long life expectancy, they may be from about age 40 to 60 and beyond. Some researchers have the middle years start at age 50, maybe even 60. In societies with low life expectancy (the late 40s), the middle years could be the early 30s. You decide what your middle years are.

In *Christian Life Patterns: The Psychological Challenges and Religious Invitations of Adult Life*, Evelyn Eaton Whitehead and James D. Whitehead write that psychologically, the mid-years are marked by the dominance of three interwoven themes: personal power, care, and interiority.

Personal power: The middle-aged person wants and needs to be effective in the tasks that define his or her work. It's a time when you come into your own as a human being. You know who you are and what you are capable of. You have a better sense of mastery of your life. This is the time your dream as a young adult becomes a reality.

Care: To mature, you need the experience of others being dependent on you, of being taken care of by you. When you are an adult, you are willing and ready to be saddled with the care of children. Caring is rooted in awareness of personal power. In the middle years, you have more discretionary money, so you can now give it away or spend it in broader social concerns. You have proven skills, so you can use them in some venture that will count. You have time and energy.

You can contribute to church and community programs and causes. You have a strong sense of self-identity. You can stand up and lead neglected or set-aside causes. You have readiness to mentor young people.

Interiority: As the mid-life person continues to move outward with an increasing interior stock-taking and exploring the world within, he or she develops a heightened sensitivity to self and an increasing focus on inner needs.

Middle adulthood is not usually a plateau, but a movement toward growth and change. Toward the end of this period most people become aware of their mortality and that they may have fewer years ahead of them than they already have lived. Retirement lies ahead, which may mean new social roles, financial changes, and changes in living patterns and work loads. For a long time during this period I had a hand-lettered sign on my desk: "What do I want to do before I die?" not out of a sense of morbidity, but because time was rushing past me. It said, "Get with it, Katie. You haven't got forever."

As you continue working on your life story, keep gathering everything you can find, such as diaries, photographs, home videos, mementos. Keep talking to family members and friends. Your questions will arouse interest in them. Look for anecdotes, nicknames, celebrations, and so forth.

Try to put your finger on the emotional climate of your own home during this period. Were there periods of anxiety, despair, frustration?

Were there periods of relative calm and peacefulness? What caused these changes in atmosphere? Was it some prolonged family problem or something caused by circumstances beyond your control when the regular flow of time was broken by a crisis? As I've said, it's important to get comfortable with your own life story — its bumps, diversions, uphill struggles, and downhill slides. It's your story. It's important to you and those coming after you.

Examine the following expected and unexpected life changes that usually take place in middle adulthood:

Expected life changes	Unexpected life changes
Raising a family (and living happily ever after)	Loss of spouse through death or divorce
Children marrying	Loss of identity and role
Becoming grandparents	Children's divorce
Death of parents	Delinquent children
Work in church/community	Financial instability/failure/success
Making friends	Responsibility for a parent
Empty nest	Return of children to home in later life
Volunteer work	Illness of child or spouse
Being the wage earner	Physical changes and illnesses
	Learning to use modern technology
	Returning to school
	Finding a different church home
	Losing a home or job
	Discovery of a new talent or skill

Make your own list. An account of these expected and unexpected transitions will be a different story than an autobiography about travels, houses, and belongings you amassed, or degrees you completed. Think through your emotions as you examine each item. How did you handle the transition? Was it smooth or uncomfortable? What challenges did you face? What new lessons did you learn?

Some people are devastated when their youngest child leaves home. I admit I felt ambivalent, elated, and sad, when my son finally decided he could survive in the dormitory three blocks down the street as well as at home. The empty nest syndrome is likely to become a crisis only for women who have identified their role exclusively with the family and its maintenance. When does it become a problem for fathers? What resources did you find to help you or did you gut it out?

WRITING OPTION:

Choose one transition or change you faced in your middle years. Tell the story honestly and candidly, explaining how you faced it or ran away.

Stage 5: Retirement and Beyond

In her bestselling book *Passages*, Gail Sheehy writes about adult transitions. Even as there are stages in development throughout one's entire life, so there are stages within each stage. Becoming an adult has stages. Becoming an older adult also has these different levels.

You can't dump everyone over the age of 60 into one age group labeled "old" anymore. One day you wake up and find there is an 80-year-old woman in your spot in bed. But that woman isn't the same person who was there 10 years before. With today's improved medical care, people are living well into their 80s and 90s. And they are changing and continuing to reach for new horizons as they grow older. Many of them will spend more years in retirement than they did in the work force.

So we need to think of the young-old, the middle-old, and the old-old, sometimes referred to as the frail-old. The needs and expectations differ with each of these late-life stages. The question for us is what does it mean to be in each life stage? What should we write about in our 60s, 70s, and 80s, or beyond? It is rich, virgin territory.

The young-old are often considered to be the newly retired. Whereas my parents, and possibly yours, saw retirement as a kind of retreat (moving to the rocking chair), today's young-old think of retirement as re-treading, or regrouping, and plunging ahead into life again. Respond as quickly as possible to the following questions to clarify your attitudes toward this stage.

1. What do you think of the terms "senior citizen" or "golden ager"?

2. Why does the word "old" upset some people?

3. What is your general image of aging?

4. What is the best part of being an older person in our society?
Consider the following:
   - Freedom from the alarm clock
   - Freedom to wear low-heel shoes
   - Being able to look over your whole life and acknowledge
     what has happened
   - Better understanding of what gives life meaning
   - Recognizing that accumulating things lacks significance
   - Finding personal relationships more important
   - Release from some demanding responsibilities
   - Enjoying new opportunities for volunteer work
   - Relishing opportunities to revive old interests and develop
     new ones
   - Experiencing an unusual awareness of your own wisdom
   - Readiness to acknowledge the possibility of inner growth
   - A new awareness of the challenge of being a role model
   - The opportunity to develop a new identity

5. What don't you like about this life stage?
   - Decline of physical strength and health
   - Being on a fixed income
   - Changes in living arrangements

- Possible loss of a spouse, parent, child, or friends to death
- Nearness to the end of life
- Dependence on others, particularly family
- Having to face past failures
- The challenge of dealing with inertia and meaninglessness

6. What did you expect would happen after retirement?
   - Travel
   - Recreation, such as golf
   - Volunteer work
   - More free time
   - Grandparenting
   - Hobbies

Soon after moving to Wichita, Kansas, following retirement I volunteered for an organization, but grew weary of the director, who spent the first half hour to 45 minutes of every meeting scolding the volunteers for not doing enough. I decided I did not need this at this stage of my life, so I moved on to a hospice organization. I enjoyed my work as a hospice volunteer, but finally resigned because I did not like having to find new addresses in the city, being directionally challenged. I get lost frequently and in all settings. I moved on to test other organizations and finally settled on the East Wichita Shepherd's Center, where I could be myself as I taught writing classes with freedom and joy.

7. What did you *not* plan on happening after retirement? Consider
    the following:

- Death of a child or spouse or caring for an ill child or spouse
- Taking full care of grandchildren
- Loss of health, hair, or other changes in physical appearance
- Changes in friends
- Changes in identity
- Facing one's mortality
- Greater freedom to be yourself
- Loss or increase in income
- Changes in residence
- Losing car keys or checkbook
- Spiritual doubts and fears
- Changes in attitudes toward possessions
- Learning to use new technology
- Joy in volunteering
- Renewal of creative talents and gifts
- Freedom to push a cause or wave a flag

As you review your own retirement years, the above questions
should give you many topics to write about. What is the difference
between the person you are now and the person you were decades ago?
List five or six critical decisions you made in your life. Think of actual
decisions, such as returning to school, learning to use a computer,
deciding to forgive someone, moving from one place to another, changing religious or political persuasions, or shifting from racism to greater

tolerance. Think through your feelings as you look at each decision. Only the elderly can assure younger generations that life has meaning at every stage, even when you are heading toward the end. If the image of aging is negative, all society loses. What wisdom embodied in stories do you want to pass on?

WRITING OPTION:

Write about some event that happened in your retirement years that had significant meaning for you, such as facing reduced income or a change in your physical condition. How did your spouse react to your retirement? One friend told her newly retired husband she had married him for better or for worse, but not for lunch every day. Consequently, he had to find a place to eat lunch. As a result, he ended up volunteering at places or joining organizations where they served lunch. How did you deal with not having to go to work each day? How did you find a volunteer job? What have been your experiences as a volunteer?

HISTORY HAPPENS
TO EVERYONE

Personal history is always influenced by your family history, and family history is always part of national and social history. We are shaped by our times with both short and long-term effects. You want to retrieve how you and your family were affected in attitude and practice by the events of history.

You can't really understand an 80-year-old without addressing how that person was affected by the Great Depression, any more than you can understand those who lived during World War II without learning how conscription, rationing, and other economic and social factors affected them. Major social and political events shape lives more than we realize. They change direction and goals. During the Depression era, men with advanced degrees dug ditches and took to the rails, if need be. During nearly every war, marriage, education, and other dreams have had to be postponed. If your family was part of a strong church community, that congregation and the denomination it belonged to also were changed by historical events, following societal drifts.

If you haven't already done so, make a grid or timeline of your life (see page 28, Exercise 2). Add details you discover in this unit to it.

Echoes of the Great Depression

Chuck Underwood, generational marketing strategy speaker, points out that during our formative years we form core values for life. Those who lived at the same time share values, motivations, and attitudes. Marketers win if they recognize that these core values shape decisions like consumer spending. My generation, who grew up during the Depression, has that experience indelibly stamped on its psyche. It continues to influence us to this day. I am still always conscious of food waste, the need to reuse and recycle, and the awareness that a healthy economy does not last forever. Move through the following questions as quickly as possible, noting events that come to mind easily.

1. Where were you or your parents living when the stock market of 1929 crashed?

2. Did your family lose anything in the crash? Do you know anyone who did? How did it affect them? Think of instances of renewed

courage to continue, but also clinical depression, despair, suicide, and increased isolation.

3. Did your parents have a job or steady income during the Great Depression?

4. What changed in your family lifestyle? Daily routines? Clothing purchases?

5. Did your family have trouble making ends meet?

6. What main stories about this period, both humorous and sad, are told and retold? Did your family experience the terrible Dust Bowl years?

     A class member told this story of this era:

> Faye recalled an incident when her father lost the farm during the Dust Bowl days in western Kansas. The family was forced to move to another farm, and he walked to work to town a distance away to earn a small wage. The winds blew dust through every crack in the aging wooden frame house so that it piled up against inside baseboards and on window sills.
>
> The family was large, so when the cow went dry because of lack of feed, Faye's mother was desperate to know what to feed her baby. Daily, her father stopped off at

a neighboring farm to pick up a small pail of milk. But one afternoon when the dust blew so thick, night arrived while it was still day, and her father did not come home from work. Faye said they couldn't see the barn from the house. Had he lost his way in the darkness?

The oldest son, about 12, begged his mother to let him search for his father. He would use his new five-battery flashlight. He would be sure to find him. Her mother wavered. She couldn't go herself and leave her large brood alone at home. Supposing she also got lost? Finally, against her better judgment, she let the young boy venture into the growing darkness, armed only with his flashlight and childhood bravery. She and the children waited and waited in the unnatural gloom lit only by a kerosene lamp. Finally, the door burst open, the son leading his father, eyes and nostrils crusted with dirt. In his hand he clung to the little red pail of milk.

As I heard Faye tell the story of her father's courage and her mother's trust in her son, I wished the audience had been young people instead of mostly those over the age of 70, who knew such courage from their own experiences.

7. Do you or your parents remember breadlines or hobos riding the rails? Here's a friend's story:

John felt the need to earn more than he could in Minnesota, so he decided to go West during the Depression. He hopped freight trains and headed across the Dakotas and Montana. Montana gave him a good story to tell his grandchildren. Here he was arrested for vagrancy. A policeman took him and several others to the jail house where they were told they were free to leave if they paid $20 each. A couple of the guys paid and left. The next day the policeman told the rest they could go for $10, probably sensing these were men with less money. More paid and left. And so it went with the ante coming down each day. Soon only a couple of men were left.

The officer said, "You'll have to go to jail if you can't give me any money."

"I'll give you everything in my pocket," answered John, which was about 27 cents. The officer took it and John walked out, feeling the texture of the $20 bill in his sock and his integrity intact.

8. What about foreclosures on loans? How did people respond to such events?

9. Do you or your parents remember when Roosevelt closed all the banks in 1932?

10. Were people happy despite being without money? How did they find entertainment? Consider sandlot games, movies, board games, parlor games, radio, mystery novels. Why did Monopoly become a popular game during this time? What kinds of movies appealed to people the most during this difficult time?

11. Consider the following statistics for the years 1930-39, taken from the Internet:

> **U.S. population:** 123,188,000
> **Life expectancy:** Males 58.1, females 61.6
> **Average annual salary:** $1,368
> **Unemployment:** 25 percent
> **Number of car sales:** 2,787,400
> **Prices:** Milk 14 cents a quart, bread 9 cents,
> round steak 42 cents

Why was life expectancy lower then than now? What contributed to it? How did this affect your family?

12. What happened when people got sick but had no money?

Stories about homesteading on the prairies have a special poignancy because of the desperation that drove the settlers. In one of the first classes I taught on writing life stories, Edna, then in her 80s, offered this story, which she wanted her children and grandchildren to remember:

Edna's parents lived on a dry land farm in Oklahoma. Somehow a board fell into the well from which they got all their water, contaminating it. How to get it out? Her parents decided that three-year-old Edna would be lowered into the well in a large pail with a bale handle to retrieve it. Her father was too heavy for her mother to pull out and for some reason lowering her mother was not an option.

They experimented first on dry ground with Edna in the pail, but the bale handle flopped over too easily, tipping Edna out. So her father fixed that problem and they lowered her into the deep darkness of the well. Her little hands were too small to grab the slippery board. They pulled her up, deliberated some more, and then lowered her again with new instructions. Her parents were desperate. They had to have water. She grabbed that board and clung to it until she was safe in the arms of her waiting parents. Eight decades later, she still remembered the horror of the moment at the bottom of the well, groping in the darkness for a slippery board.

Here are other elements to consider in writing about the Depression years.

Transportation: What are the various modes of transportation you have experienced? Consider horse and buggy, walking, bicycle, car, train, airplane, boat. Do you remember your first airplane ride? What about the first time you saw an airplane?

Communication: Letters, telegraph, telephone, etc. Do you remember receiving a telegram from someone? What kind of feeling was associated with telegrams in your early years? Can you remember your family's first radio? Did you own a crystal radio set? Why did boys find them so attractive to build from kits?

When did you see your first TV show? What were some of the early shows? How do they differ from today's programs? Did your family subscribe to a newspaper or magazine? What were they? Who read them? When did newsletters become popular?

Entertainment: Chautauqua tent gatherings, lantern slides, reel movies, home-produced drama, radio, parlor and sandlot games, marbles, jackknives, skipping rope, playing jacks, etc.

WRITING OPTION:

Write a story about some aspect of the social environment you were familiar with during your early years. Move slowly through your story, trying to get as close to the essence of the story as possible. When did it happen? To whom? What strong emotion did you remember that permeated the household at the time? Was it related to lack of money, food, disagreements in the family, or joy in the midst of need?

WRITING TIPS:

1. *Relive an early experience in your mind. Move as close to it as you can.*

2. *Write down all the facts about the experience as truthfully as you can. Don't write to impress the reader.*

3. *Remember that to write "I was excited" or "I found that experience interesting" does not convey the same feeling of excitement or enthusiasm to the reader. This can only be conveyed through the facts you choose to reveal.*

4. *Don't let the reader lose sight of you out of a false sense of modesty. You are the main character in your story. You must assume that your readers (such as children and grandchildren) will be interested in your story primarily because the narrative concerns you. They want to see you as a living, breathing person. In her story, Edna wanted the other class members to know this was her story.*

Exploring the Resources of World War II

> The reflections of older people on wars or hard times
> or financial insecurity are crucial to helping younger
> people cope with their own times of personal and cultural
> stress. Communicating this experience is a truly important,
> immediately useful, and deeply needed function that only the
> older generations can perform for the younger generations.
>
> –William Fletcher in *Recording Your Family History*

Here are questions frequently asked when discussing World War II. For more information, research the cultural history of the United States online. Or consider similar questions about the Vietnam War, the war in Iraq, or the war in Afghanistan.

1. Where were you the day the Japanese attacked Pearl Harbor in 1941? What did you feel? Who was with you? What did you talk about immediately afterward?

2. Where were you when the atomic bombs fell on Hiroshima and Nagasaki, Japan in 1945? Who was with you? What did you do? What were your immediate reactions? Did people understand the real significance of the event? Consider my experience:

> When I was vacationing in northern Saskatchewan at a
> resort near Prince Albert far from civilization, an acquain-

tance with a car radio urged my friends and me to join him in the car. Something earth-shaking was happening. He opened the doors wide so more people could crowd around to hear the grim news. I don't remember what we said, only the sense of knowing something mind-boggling had happened. The first atom bomb had fallen. We sat in stunned silence.

3. What were the Americans and other Allied forces fighting for? Is there a difference between that war and the war that followed the invasion of Iraq? What did it mean to defeat fascism?

4. How were you or family members involved in the war? Consider military service, Red Cross volunteer work, victory gardens, meatless days, and the rationing of gas, food, tires, and shoes.

My mother was a Red Cross volunteer, knitting dozens of socks, mittens, and scarves for the military from khaki-colored wool. She was an excellent knitter; some other women weren't. She brought home stacks of poorly-knitted socks, which would not have fit the strangest circus freak of the times, ripping them and turning the heel to her satisfaction and the prospective recipient's comfort.

5. What was the feeling in the country during this time? How was the feeling maintained by the government?

6. Did you or your family members become Rosie-the-Riveters? During World War II, an unprecedented number of American women responded to government encouragement to enter the high-paying world of the war-production industry using the slogan, "We can do it." What kind of backgrounds did these women come from? What drew the women into the factories? How was patriotism used to dictate women's behavior? What did propaganda films say that drew them? What did women get out of war work?

7. During the Depression, married women were told not to take jobs from unemployed men. Often they were not hired. During the war, single and married women went off to work to replace men who joined the military. What happened when the troops came home from overseas? What were the women encouraged to do then? Some women never accepted that some jobs were for men only and some for women. Once having stepped over the line into men's work, they never looked back.

> As Carol Hymowitz and Michaele Weissman wrote in *A History of Women in America*:
>> Six million women took paying jobs during the War. The proportion of women in the labor force increased from 25 to 36 percent. Two million of these women went to work in offices – half of these for the federal government, handling the flow of paper created by the war. An even greater number of women went into the factories. Heavy industry

alone created nearly two million jobs for women during the war.

Two months after V–J Day 800,000 workers, most of them women, lost jobs in the aircraft industry. . . . Such companies as IBM and Detroit Edison resurrected their prewar policy against hiring married women. By the end of 1946, a million women had been fired from heavy industry. . . . After five years of keeping the war production lines moving, women were suddenly told that the work was too heavy for them.

8. Did any family members or close friends die or become injured in the war? Did they die in vain? Think about later reaction to those who returned from the Vietnam War.

9. When did you or your family members first hear about concentration camps overseas? During World War II, Japanese people were interned in camps in the inland United States. Many lost all property, personal freedoms, and educational opportunities. Were you or your family member aware of this? How did it affect you? Americans of German descent also were mistreated, but to a lesser degree. Did you know this?

10. What changed in the life of your family because of the war?

11. Which World War II-era songs, movies, or slang do you remember?

In the following incident, I unexpectedly connected with someone who experienced the war in a concentration camp, or gulag, in the Soviet Union during and after the war.

In 1989, I joined a Tabor College tour group for a trip to the country of origin of many of the tour members' parents and grandparents – the former Soviet Union. In Novisibirsk, in Siberia, a city of about six million, our group worshiped together with a small group of believers in a modest-looking building. I noticed that the hymnals were all handwritten and hand-bound. This congregation had endured much suffering.

After the service, I mentioned again to our tour leader that I wanted to return to our hotel to meet a cousin whom I had never met. The local church leader asked his flock if anyone had time to take Frau Wiebe back to her hotel. An older man immediately volunteered to escort me. I assumed he was a longtime member of the congregation and well-known to the local people. Together we traveled by streetcar a long distance. He dropped a few kopeks into the fare box as we entered, over my protestations. I spoke a little German, and he was a native speaker of German and Russian.

At a transfer intersection, he suggested we stop at a nearby park. I didn't want to, but agreed. In the little park, he carefully unfolded his handkerchief on the bench before I sat down. He gave me an account of his life – many years

in a gulag as a political prisoner. Everything I had read in
Alekhsandr Solzhenitsyn's *One Day in the Life of Ivan Denisovich*
he had experienced and recorded in a manuscript. He was
also a poet and took some poems out of a pocket to read
to me, an English professor and writer from the United
States. I was getting increasingly anxious to get back to
the hotel. What would I say if he asked me to smuggle
his manuscript out with me when I returned to Kansas? I
insisted we return. He was in no hurry.

I was shocked to learn he was not a member of the
church we had just left, having attended only a few times.
My heart was beginning to miss beats. I was in the middle
of a huge city, without Russian language skills, now at
the mercy of this unknown man who had probably been
without female companionship for decades. Finally, when I
demanded we return, he said he wanted to give me something to remember him by. His clothes were threadbare.
He offered me his comb with a few teeth missing. I refused,
for he needed it and I had many combs. Finally I suggested he give me a few kopeks, the lowest currency in the
Soviet Union. I put them in my purse and we continued
our streetcar journey, arriving at my hotel with little time
to spare. I felt relieved. I had misjudged him. He was just
hungry for companionship.

At the door, I turned to offer him my hand in farewell
and thanks. Instead he looked soulfully at me and asked,

"Wollen wir uns kuessen?" ("Why not kiss?") I gulped, and gave
him a quick peck on the cheeks before heading for the
winding staircase. I turned to wave my hand like British
royalty. My cousin was waiting in my room.

Exploring the Resources
of the Turbulent 1960s

This decade is sometimes referred to as the Swinging '60s, even as
the previous decade was known as the Silent '50s. This was a turbulent decade. John F. Kennedy, Lyndon B. Johnson, and Richard Nixon
were the American presidents. The Vietnam War, the unpopular conflict that ended formally in 1975, dominated the news as did student
uprisings, anti-war sit-ins, draft dodgers, and conscientious objectors.
Pictures of the Kent State shooting in 1970 were etched in everyone's
mind.

Youth culture radicalism moved in with the hippies and the Sexual
Revolution, opposition to "The Establishment," the Woodstock festival, the "British Invasion" in popular music, folk music, folk rock and
blues, the "generation gap," the rise of Eastern religions, and the 1967
"Summer of Love" in San Francisco. It was a new era.

Here are some other events, issues, and organizations that moved
to the forefront in this decade: the Peace Corps, the reforms of the
Vatican II council in the Roman Catholic Church, psychedelic drugs,

marijuana, the rise of the birth-control pill, feminism and gay rights, the Civil Rights movement and legislation, Martin Luther King Jr., and nonviolent resistance, Black Power, and the Black Panthers. Think also about the assassinations of John F. Kennedy (1963), Malcolm X (1965), Robert Kennedy (1968) and Martin Luther King Jr. (1968).

Mark all items of which you or your family member had personal knowledge, interest, or experience. As you think back to this decade, what general feelings move to the top?

Another approach is to list beside each year of the 1960s (or later decades) where you were, how old you were, what you were doing, who was with you, which events you know about, and which you participated in, if only in spirit.

Did you ever take sides on any unpopular issue such as civil rights or women's liberation? What did you think about the civil rights movement when people started demonstrating and demanding equal treatment of the races?

Many people thought the Vietnam War was wrong and did not believe in fighting it. Did you ever demonstrate against this war, or later wars?

Did the sexual revolution affect your thinking or actions?

If you are Catholic, how did you or your family react to the Vatican II reforms? Some Protestant groups experienced a renewal movement. This also was the start of communalism in some denominations and changes in attitudes toward church structures.

Do you know anyone who died because of a lack of antibiotics? What do you remember about the polio scare in the 1950s? What was the first reaction of people to the new "wonder drugs"? Can you remember home health visits by the doctor?

My boyfriend in the Air Force thoughtfully brought me a bottle of penicillin nose drops when I was about 18 and sick with a bad cold. He had gotten it from the base dispensary and wanted to help me get well quickly with this wonder drug. I don't remember if it helped because I got over the cold as usual.

Did your family own a record player? What replaced it? When you hear songs today that you enjoyed in the 1950s and 1960s, do they still give you a warm, fuzzy feeling about a certain time in your life or a specific person?

What clothing fashions do you remember? Hairstyles? Can you remember any incidents with your parents regarding differing opinions about hair or clothing styles like this student writer did?

Most adolescents react resentfully to depersonalization. I was no exception when my father attempted to set in my mind the older generation's tradition of a conventional, conformed hair length. I felt strongly that I was old enough to decide for myself, as an individual, the care of my property.

As a typical parent, my father was hurt deeply that his one and only son was rejecting even one value with which he had brought me up. He obviously sensed a necessity to defend his words just as I refused to back down from my convictions. Words did not satisfy the tempers of our discord and soon our lack of communication exploded into a hand–to–hand struggle.

Cluster by cluster, my hair was falling among tears. I was infuriated! For me, the whole young generation had lost a major battle against tyranny. Humiliation was descending upon my shoulders like boulders. I felt depersonalized, for my own opinion had been spat upon.

WRITING OPTION:

In writing about the 1960s, you will possibly find that your attitude toward some of the above topics has changed and that the passage of time has brought a new perspective. It's hard to admit to early strong attitudes and opinions truthfully about political, social, moral, and religious issues. We tend to forget their force or influence on us at the time. It is better to say, "I came to a new understanding" about racism, for example, than to deny it. Good memoirs are about change, not about a static life.

Exploring the Resources of the
1970s and Following Decades

Major trends during the 1970s were growing disillusionment with government, advances in civil rights legislation and affirmative action, increased influence of the women's movement, dismay at the Kent State massacre, interest in the Watergate scandal, and the rise of dual-career marriages, with both husbands and wives as wage earners.

Remember these? Mandatory busing, the Rubik's Cube, smiley face stickers, Pet Rocks, leisure suits, the Roe vs. Wade decision, the People's Temple mass suicide in Guyana, the death of Elvis Presley, and a popular interest in genealogy because of Alex Haley's book *Roots*.

Keep exploring the next decades in the same way, using the Internet to refresh your memory. Think through your involvement with major trends during this period: Binge-buying and the growing popularity of credit cards, video games, aerobics, camcorders, talk shows, the AIDS epidemic, the fall of the Berlin Wall, and changes in basic family patterns with more couples living together and more single-parent families.

> My neighbor's son had AIDS during the mid–1980s, although she did not have freedom to tell me until after his death. In the early years of this illness, few admitted to the disease because of its stigma. No one knew how it was transmitted. In those confusing times, small local hospitals

refused to treat AIDS patients, so he stayed in a Texas hospital. When he was near death, she traveled to Texas from Kansas to be with him. In the large city hospital, she was firmly instructed not to touch her son because of danger of infection, but her mother-love won out. "Katie, I reached out my hand and put it on his," she told me later. "I couldn't help myself."

Her story reminded me of an event that catapulted my childhood community of Blaine Lake in northern Saskatchewan back into Bible times. This was 20th-century Canada, but the past has ways of grabbing hold of our shirt-tails and dragging us back.

Boris and his sister, Nadya, came to Canada from Russia, near the Turkish border, in the 1920s. Even after both married, the two families continued to live together in the same little house on a piece of land they farmed jointly. In many ways, their life continued as it had in Russia.

Boris, though a quiet man, often spoke with Dad about the privileges of living in Canada. He had seen what an oppressive regime could do to personal freedom. He had a good farm, a hard-working wife, and good friends. His lines (as the Psalm says) had fallen in pleasant places. How-ever, he was troubled about an unattractive skin condition he'd had for years. If he could find a cure for it, he would enjoy life to the full.

One winter, colder than usual, the rash appeared to worsen, and Boris' wife persuaded him to see the local doctor, an Englishman, probably Dr. Warren, who spoke no Russian and wasn't able to get much medical history from Boris. He gave him a thorough examination but remained puzzled by the strange, whitish, but painless condition of the man's extremities. Finally, he attributed it to frostbite, the most logical condition for a farmer working outside with animals in a cold climate. The doctor gave Boris a mild oint-ment and assured him the rash would improve. But it didn't.

Shortly after Christmas, a new doctor and his family moved to town. They spoke several Slavic languages and dialects the people of our area used. He and his wife, also a medical doctor, had fled Russia via China. It had taken many months to get the necessary papers to migrate to Canada. While they waited, they kept busy helping the sick. They saw diseases they had never seen before – some as old as history itself. Leprosy was a common sight on the streets of the Chinese city where they lived. Deformed beggars stumbled along. Some leprosaria were overfilled with victims of this strange disease.

Shortly after Dr. Batanoff arrived in Blaine Lake in 1928, he joined the group of men who regularly gathered around the floor register in the middle of the OK Economy Store and happened to notice Boris' deformed hands. They looked strangely like the hands of a leper. Not wanting to alarm Boris and yet anxious to have his suspicions confirmed or proven false, he asked him to drop in at his office before he left for home. Boris, feeling fairly good at the time, wasn't anxious to pay another's doctor's fee, so he refused. Dr. Batanoff told him there would be no charge; he was merely interested in Boris' hands for personal reasons and wanted to do a few tests. A biopsy was performed that afternoon and sent to the Department of Health in Regina. Then everything exploded at once in our quiet little village.

The Royal Canadian Mounted Police were dispatched to Boris' home and a huge red quarantine sign nailed on the door, much bigger than the kind placed on our door when we had measles. A guard allowed no one to enter or leave. Within a few days, a special Canadian National Railroad car, well marked with quarantine signs, was parked on the siding near town. Though it was the dead of winter and bitterly cold, plans to move the leper and his family to a leprosarium off the eastern coast of Canada were executed with dispatch.

Early one morning, while it was still dark, a strange procession moved through town to the quarantined railroad car. The two couples, their parents, and a few belongings were crowded into one sleigh hitched to another sleigh like a trailer by means of long leather straps so that no one had to get close to the infected man. A full contingent of RCMP guarded the procession.

Once they had left, their possessions were inventoried and their furniture burned. The house was fumigated and all farm buildings treated with lime.

Earlier, Dad and Dr Batanoff had made up a grocery list sufficient to supply six people with food for six days, packed the food into cartons, and took them to the train car. We, of course, got the full impact of this gripping drama from Dad. This unclean disease of leprosy belonged in Jesus' time, not ours.

My sister Frieda looked through our limited school library for information about leprosy, for she wanted to be a nurse, but could find nothing. For weeks thereafter, she said she examined our hands and feet, fearful we might have numb white patches, for she had handled Boris' money in the store.

Boris and his family were taken across Canada by train to an island off the coast of Newfoundland. The freedom Boris had been so grateful for was suddenly gone. For years, nothing was heard of this family. Then one day, the sister's husband and Boris' wife returned to Blaine Lake. They had been certified clean and could resume a normal life. Boris also came back briefly but returned to the island, for he had made friends there. His sister converted to Catholicism and died at the leprosarium.

My sister Frieda Schroeder, in particular, helped with this story. I was too young to remember much.

Here's another experience I had that involved political attitudes during the 1980s and '90s.

Toward the end of the Cold War in 1989, and the end of my stay in the former Soviet Union, I felt a tremendous sigh of relief when I passed Russian customs. As a tour group, we were always under the supervision of Russian guides and were not permitted to travel freely. Even requesting special permission didn't give us what we asked for.

The rest of the tour group left before I did for the United States and Canada. I planned to stop off in Germany, so I had to manage Russian customs myself. Just before I left, my Russian cousin's husband gave me a pint jar of caviar that he and some friends had made, saying, "It's illegal to export more than 250 grams at a time." This jar contained at least 500 grams or more. "I don't think I can take it across," I remonstrated. He insisted it was his gift. "Give it to the custom official if there's a problem," he suggested, quite nonchalantly, knowing the people of his country better than I did.

At the border, with the contraband caviar deep in my suitcase, my heart shuddered when the official motioned me to open my suitcase after looking at the image on the X-ray screen. I obeyed. I had visions of sitting in a harsh Soviet jail in Siberia by myself for the rest of my life, living on bread and water. He dug deeply into my suitcase while looking at the screen. Finally, he pulled out my jewelry case (which held nothing but costume jewelry) and pulled out a little metal scarf ring. He examined it briefly, "Not gold," he muttered. He looked at the few kopeks my poet friend had given me and replaced them. He motioned that I could close my suitcase. My ordeal was over. The caviar and I had made it through customs. And I don't even like caviar.

Keep looking for those times when your life intersected with major historical events. History happens to everyone.

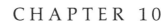

MEMORIES ARE ALSO MADE OF THESE

The Works of Our Lives

Although our personal development is an inner process, the evidence of it is quite outward. I will call that evidence of the inner life "work." According to Ira Proghoff, author of a seminal book on journaling, "A work is a specific project that emerges as an outer activity drawn from an inner source in a person's life."

In simpler terms, the inner life needs an outward form or "work" to fulfill it. A person with a musical bent needs an outlet or a "work" to develop and use those musical talents. A person who likes to dig in the soil and grow stuff needs an acre or more to release that inner tension. The compulsion to play a musical instrument, to quilt, to grow vegetables comes from deep within, not by someone standing over you with a stick saying, "Do this, or else!"

So "work" is anything to which you have dedicated yourself because it gave — or gives — meaning to your life. Something inside compelled you to keep doing it. A work is something that has great inner meaning for you. A job is something you do because you have to.

WRITING OPTION:

Go back to your original grid with the eight divisions (see page 28, Exercise 2). Under each division list the works you were involved in at the time. It might have been making mud pies as a preschooler, playing on a school ball team in grade school, doing "dangerous" experiments in science in high school, becoming an activist for some cause in young adulthood, or playing golf as an older adult. Over the years, you may have dropped some works because you outgrew them, rejected them, or replaced them with others. In your list, include works you wanted to do during a specific period and didn't or couldn't because of circumstances. Include those carried over from the past to the present.

Now trace the history of one of the works you have listed. You may have been a tennis enthusiast from grade school through college, winning tournaments by the dozen. Others saw it as an athletic outlet. You did it because you had to. You had no other option. How did you get started in tennis? Was it peer pressure? The influence

of your elders or other people? Reading about tennis greats such as
Arthur Ashe? If you gave it up, when and why?

As a teenager I wanted desperately to make my fingers fly over the piano keys but only could plunk out a few simple songs. I wanted to take piano lessons but lacked the resources. Dad liked guitar and mandolin music, the kind he grew up with in Russia. He couldn't handle slow practicing, one painful wrong note after another. Piano music was too thin and plinky.

I bartered with him. I would work in the store on Saturdays for music lessons – one half-hour lesson every other week. And I would never practice when he was in the house, or on Sunday. When he was around, I would only play music he could appreciate. Also, I would learn one new hymn each lesson. Fair enough. Dad agreed. The deal was made.

I got paid for working in the store, 75 cents each Saturday, to pay for lessons. So every two weeks for several years, I trotted next door to the home of Mrs. Phyllis Davidson for a half-hour lesson, working my way through each book diligently and swiftly. She encouraged, she inspired. Dad gradually accepted piano playing, and I eventually took exams in performance, history, and harmony.

During my high school years, I pounded the piano by the hour, pouring out my soul through all kinds of music, including contemporary popular songs. A few touched me to the core, but I had no money to buy sheet music. This was the late 1930s, when the Depression still held a strong grip on society. Ever resourceful, I borrowed sheet music from friends and bought paper scored for music. With pen and India ink I copied page after page of musical scores, ignorant of copyright laws. Now I had my own music. As I look at these carefully copied pieces of music, I wonder at the passion of that girl and her need to play romantic popular music. Was it simply due to a dearth of varieties of music in our home?

When I attended college several years later, I continued taking lessons but soon realized I was neither a virtuoso pianist nor a performer. And I couldn't play by ear, a skill much in demand in church settings.

After marriage, I continued to play for our children as they stomped in circles around the house, and listened to records of classical piano music with my husband late at night. Mozart's *Eine Kleine Nachtmusik* was a favorite. When I began freelance writing, I no longer had time nor interest in playing the piano. My passion, my work, became writing.

What did you learn about yourself from this exercise? As I reviewed my interest in piano playing, I came up with incident after incident related to music and pianos in my childhood home, enough to write a chapter in my book, The Storekeeper's Daughter.

You can apply the same exercise to any "work" in your life or someone else's if you are writing a biography. Find its genesis and then keep adding detail after detail related to its growth. Some "works" stay with us into later years, others get phased out. There's always a reason, and it's up to you to find it.

In my young son's life, the summer of the spaceship (or was it a rocket?) stands out in my mind. First was born in his seven-year-old head the idea of building his own model spaceship. For several days, the idea incubated with occasional mutterings to the rest of the family about the scientific wonder about to hit the headlines. Sketches were penciled on paper. Then came a period of salvaging building materials, mostly tin cans, interrupted by repeated frustration for him when forgetful sisters and Mother kept dumping his cans into the trash.

When he had finally collected enough cans, the moment arrived for his architectural drawings to become reality. This was, however, the moment of deepest despair. I, chief assistant engineer, was too ignorant of spaceships to be helpful. Nor did I know enough about using tools. A project capable of changing the course of scientific history seemed doomed to permanent failure; humankind might never know another Sputnik.

Somehow Jamie's plight came to the attention of our older friend, Mr. Jost. One Saturday morning, he dropped in to find Jamie distraught. He packed Jamie, tin cans, and drawings into his truck and left for the day. The happiest boy in the world came home that evening carrying a large monstrosity of welded tin cans because this older man had helped him weld vital building material into something he had thought up himself.

Years later, James and his friend, Marlin, built a computer port contender for the offices of a college consortium. The contract stipulated a minimum of seven days problem-free operation in exchange for $5,000, huge money for a pair of penniless freshmen. They had never done this before, but they thought they could produce the required product. They worked far into the night for weeks with James coming home in the morning to shower and return for classes. After a few hours of sleep in the afternoon, they went at it again, and again, burning out transistors, only to have to order more from California and try again. They finished on time, and their port contender held up for seven days without a hitch as the contract required. James's early "work" of creating continued into his adult years as a computer engineer designing hardware, particularly peripheral memory devices.

Writing About the Life Others Don't See

What about experiences restricted mainly to what happens inside you – such as the moment when doubt becomes faith, or confusion lifts and clarity sets in? Perhaps you recall the moment you made a great discovery about life or found strength and courage to move out of the darkness of despair into a more constructive mood. Life went on as usual, but inside you were different. These inner events are difficult to write about because a step-by-step set of directions didn't come with the experience.

I am aware that some religious groups have tried to make it easier for adherents to describe inner religious experiences by formularizing the process of becoming a believer. For example, if you can name a place, a Bible verse, a time, or can recall a sense of conviction, or if you responded to an altar call, you have the words to describe your experience. I grew up in such a religious environment, always trying to make my spiritual experiences fit the prescribed model. It didn't work. It took me years to recognize that God doesn't work the same way in every person's life. I wrote the following in 1962 to explain how I found direction in life.

By a strange set of circumstances I found myself living in a convalescent home shortly after I left home to work in the city. I was nearly 20, entering adult life, yet a paying guest in an institution where the other residents had already lost their firm grasp on life. Perhaps it was living so close to the waning edge of life that caused me to do some serious thinking that summer.

One Saturday morning, I walked into the large, sunny reading room, hoping someone would be there to help me while away the time. It was empty. With nothing better to do I rummaged through some untidy shelves of books and papers. There I found it – the book that was to change my life. It wasn't a very exciting-looking book. A quick glance at its contents revealed no interesting conversation sprinkled here and there. I did notice it was a religious book, and I usually found it wise not to read seriously about religious stuff. It might complicate my life. But any book to read was better than nothing.

It turned out to be a volume of daily devotional readings, and so, much in the same manner I had often sought a penny fortune in a slot machine, I turned to the entry for September 1. Words of Scripture leaped from the page to arrest me: "You shall be holy, for I am holy" (I Peter 1:16 RSV). The introductory paragraph began, "Continually restate to yourself what the purpose of your life is. The destined end of man is not happiness nor health, but holiness." These were the intensely right words for me. Here was the answer to my problem. I had lacked purpose, and this book I held in my hand was telling me what that purpose was. I read eagerly to the end of the page.

That day a weak, faltering faith received strengthening, and aimless feet were put on course. A life without ambition was given a goal. A rebellious spirit yielded to a Master.

Much as I would have liked to keep the book for myself—it had no owner's name on the cover—my new concept of following Christ forbade this. I typed out a copy of the reading that had so impressed me and returned the book to the shelf in the common room. Perhaps some weary pilgrims, nearing the end of life's journey, found strength and comfort from reading that book. I did not want to rob them of it.

Several years later, a close friend gave my husband and me a copy of *My Utmost for His Highest* by Oswald Chambers as a wedding gift. When within a few weeks I came upon the familiar selection for September 1, I recognized immediately the book I thought had been lost to me forever. I rejoiced as at the return of a long-lost friend. For years I have read in it with great inspiration and help.

Your theology — or personal beliefs about God, about women's role in church and society, equality of races, and other issues — has a history of some kind. Our theology doesn't come into our lives full blown. It begins somewhere, sometimes with a small statement or experience, and evolves. Various influences are at work all the time: tradition, family and church life, church teachings, literature, movies, preaching, cultural mores, and friends.

Because the journey of faith involves the repeated correction of misconceptions, every attitude or belief you hold has a history. Every value you hold, such as generosity, honesty, punctuality, and fidelity in marriage, started somewhere, probably in your childhood. That story may be short or long.

The following exercise will help you trace the story of an inner experience much the same as you traced the history of a "work" in your life.

WRITING OPTION:

Think of some attitude, value, or belief you hold that you have changed your mind about over the years, or one that always has been present. Then list all the details and experiences related to the development of that attitude. Keep going over them. You will find yourself remembering more and more. The experiences you remember may be an encounter with few words or a glimpse of a life in a book or film. It may be the memory of regular reinforcement from parents or a teacher.

George F. Simons, in Journal for Life, *suggests drawing a graph of your experiences in terms of highs and lows to discover the texture of an inner event. Draw a line down the middle of the page with your birth at the top and the years of your life by decades or shorter intervals. Then chart your spiritual experiences from left to right as you move through your life. A peak or high point would* be recorded on the right of the center line, valleys or low points on the left.

To trace my spiritual development, I begin on the right-hand side. In early childhood, I had a simple trust in God. My line stays on the plus side because vacation Bible school was fun and mother's daily Bible stories comforting. I liked listening to her pray. But as I got a little older, my line shifted to the left because I became aware of hell and a judgmental God. I recall being terrified one night in 1932 because I had heard the world was coming to an end that night.

During my adolescence, the line shifts back and forth to show that I went forward at an altar call, but then found nothing had changed, inside or out. The line moves to the plus side again when, over a year's reflection and prayer, I committed myself to becoming a Christian. I have continued to plot my spiritual development into my middle years and beyond. It stays much more steadily on the plus side as I move into my 80s. Life is more serene.

Simons suggests as you make this graph, jot down the feelings resulting from events as you remember them. You will discover that your religious experience has had aspects that were more satisfying spiritually than others. You will discover patterns repeating themselves. Don't forget to include names of people who interacted with you. What roles did they play in your spiritual development? Once you have recorded your spiritual journey on a graph, you have a guide to writing the whole story of your spiritual development. How do you describe something as vague as a "blessing"?

Mike, a retired high school athletic instructor, had been persuaded by his wife to join a mission group going to Mexico to help at a mission. He went unconvinced he could help. His carpentry and similar skills were minimal. In high school shop class, when the instructor asked him to square a 10–inch board, he ended up with a two–by–two piece of wood. He believed he had nothing to contribute. He botched one plumbing job, so then restricted himself to safe jobs such as cleaning bathrooms, weeding, and hoeing.

At the closing public event of the group's stay in Mexico, a gathering with local people, all guest workers were called to the front. Mike humbly followed at the end of the long line of visitors, having done only lowly jobs, only to find himself in front of the group on stage. People from the local congregation heaped praise and thanks on the visitors. He felt uncomfortable. Surgeons, nurses, people with great skill, should be praised, not him. Then, suddenly, Mike said, "Grace fell on me." He became aware of God's presence and blessing upon him. It didn't matter whether he was among the highly skilled. He only knew it had been good to have been there on this mission trip doing his little bit.

At the funeral of the father of a friend, I heard another story that bears retelling. The place was packed when my daughter and I arrived, but we found the last two seats in the large auditorium.

During part of the service, the oldest daughter got up to speak. She told a story that soon hushed the large audience.

After college, she went to Nepal in volunteer service. While there, she fell in love with a Dutch doctor from Holland. They decided to get married in Nepal. Over Christmas, her parents came to visit and she and her father argued all week about who, what, and when to marry. Her father was against her marrying someone he didn't know. They parted in anger.

Before long she found she was pregnant. She sent an air gram home to her parents explaining her situation, but saying they still planned to marry.

Back came the wire: "Too hurt to respond."

Wedding plans continued.

One day as she was cycling back to her lodgings, who should she see coming up the path but her father, carrying a big suitcase in each hand.

"What are you doing here, Dad?"

"I've come to mend bridges. You are my daughter and I love you." He had brought one suitcase full of wedding gifts and one full of baby gifts.

On his way back to the United States, he stopped off in Holland to meet her future in-laws.

The woman turned to the large congregation sitting in front of her, especially the row of young teenage and young adult grandchildren, to say: "Remember, there is nothing you can do that will separate you from the love of your parents." The congregation was hushed as she finished.

She told a story about something that happens inside families. She was telling all of us that in a family, broken bridges can be mended when there is forgiveness. Stories are healing to a listener – but also to the teller. Writing the story of my widowhood gave me the freedom to let go of the hurt and accept what had happened with new courage.

Writing About Relationships
With People

A story never truly starts until it has a person or a personal pro-noun in it. "I discover who I am through exploration of all the relationships of my experiences, for I am created only in the experience of those relationships," wrote Jewish theologian Martin Buber. Do you recall reading a book with pages of description of streets and houses, vegetation and rivers, and asking: "When is the story ever going to start?" You breathe a sigh of relief when finally a person appears on the scene, if only to ask, "What's for supper?" A story needs a human being. One student I had in a six-week workshop could never allow himself to write about his relationships with people. His essays always ended with lengthy descriptions of the inanimate. Plan to write about people, especially your relationships with them.

Generally speaking, we have relationships with two kinds of people: Those with whom we have an outer relationship – a postal carrier, checkout clerk, neighbor, a stranger at the laundromat, or a plumber. The relationship is usually casual, limited, and superficial, yet sometimes these very brief casual relationships can be quite meaningful.

My neighbor for about 10 years was an older woman whose husband had died some years ago. A gentle, unassuming woman, she was a rare gift in a neighbor. One midweek afternoon, she knocked at the door carrying a plate of fresh cinnamon rolls. "What's the occasion?" I asked. Cinnamon rolls were her Saturday creations.

She had awakened that morning to realize this day was the anniversary of her wedding some 60 years ago. Her spirits drooped at the thought of spending it alone. Then she recalled the cinnamon rolls served at the wedding reception. Out came the mixing bowl, yeast, milk, and flour. She phoned friends and relatives to share her rolls to commemorate the occasion. All morning they trooped by to enjoy cinnamon rolls and memories with her. What had started out dismally became a great celebration. She wanted to share her joy with me also.

The largest proportion of relationships that have inner importance to us are those with whom we have had close and constant contact. Even after many years, you can feel the tug, either negative or positive. Think of family members, friends, students, fellow workers, a pastor, teacher, or supervisor. You will have to judge which category these people fit in by the emotional tug they have for you.

WRITING OPTION:

List about a dozen people who have been important to your life. This can include spouse, parents, children, siblings, friends, students, customers, clients, and so forth — even characters in books, authors, or celebrities. It may be someone you have never known personally, only in a distant way. They need not be alive.

After you have made your list, sort them into present and past relationships and people who are not now living. You will have three groups of people. In your eight-division grid, place the people in as many of your divisions as possible. Parents may possibly be part of all stages of life except the most recent. This exercise will give you an idea of the span of a relationship. My husband and I were married for only 15 years, which at the time of his death seemed fairly long, but from the standpoint of today was brief, too brief.

Add to each name a few phrases indicating the status of this relationship to you. Reflect your feelings about its essence: loving, hateful, generous, mean, frustrating, harmonious, supportive, or conflicted. Include changes in the relationship. If the person is dead, how do you feel about him or her now?

The past sometimes has a way of browbeating us today, turning us into victims: "My parents, teachers, religious leader, spouse, child, etc., did this to me." While this is not a therapy class, taking ownership of your whole life by objectifying it and putting it on paper is an excellent way to make peace with the past, forgive, and move on.

Next, list all the steps or events in your relationship. What do you know about the other person's life and background? When did you meet? How did this person contribute to your life? Which were important encounters?

Now tell the story of this relationship as if you are telling it to someone sitting across the table from you. Dare to acknowledge this relationship as a significant part of your life. Do not make up parts unless you intend to label it fiction at the end.

Add dialogue that is natural sounding and that might have taken place between characters. Dialogue lightens any piece of writing. I recommend not inventing long speeches for an autobiography.

In the winter of 1963, about a month after I had started working outside the home full-time for the first time, I came home at lunch to find a loaf of homemade brown bread on my table. In those days we didn't lock doors. I accepted the anonymous gift gratefully, even as I wondered about the donor.

Shortly thereafter, Mrs. Susie Jost stopped by one evening to say, "I want to do your laundry for you." Laundry for five people, four of them children? And by a stranger? I couldn't accept her gracious offer even though laundry was a big hassle. At lunch, I rushed home to load my laundry, quickly drive to the laundromat downtown when I knew many machines would be empty, fill a half dozen, rush home to eat lunch, return to gather the wet clothing, and if I had time, hang some of it on the outside line. Mrs. Jost insisted and I finally gave in.

All winter she picked up our laundry Sunday evening and returned it on prayer meeting night, neatly folded, ironed, and sometimes mended. A new towel sometimes was slipped into the pile. Mr. and Mrs. Jost became grandparents to my children for the next several years, eager to have the children come to their farm for a weekend just like their own grandchildren. At the Jost home, Christine, our third daughter who always had to share a room with her sisters, became a princess for a night with a room of her own. Mrs. Jost smiled as she told me about the first time Chris, then in grade school, lowered herself into the bed and murmured, "What luxury." So little to give a child, yet so much.

James wheedled time and love for himself from the Josts also. Loaded with lunch and fishing gear, he often biked out to the farm to spend the day at the creek. He seldom caught many fish, but it became a family joke that though he always ate the food he had brought along, he usually joined the Josts for their evening meal a little later and could see nothing incongruous about such an arrangement. Why turn down a good meal and fellowship with friends?

This warm relationship with Mr. and Mrs. John B. Jost continued until they moved to the city and later died. It was a relationship we treasured with many more warm times together.

WRITING OPTION:

Write about a person with whom you interacted at some time. Let it cover one encounter between the two of you. Keep this an "I" story and tell the reader what happened. Get as close to the story as you can.

The Best or Worst
Time of Your Life

As you keep paging through the book of your life, becoming more comfortable with all its chapters, you may quickly page over the best or worst times because they were too intense. Writing your memoir gives you the opportunity to bring joy to the present by reviewing what was good in the past and to take the edge off the worst times by looking at these experiences through more objective eyes so that they no longer hurt, bother, or disturb. You may not want to open all these experiences to public eyes, but reviewing them will give you greater control of them. Maybe you have never told anyone about some of these events. Maybe you've mentioned them too often and your children are weary of hearing your stories. Maybe it still puzzles you why a friend suddenly broke off a friendship or why your life turned out the way it did.

Author and psychologist Erich Fromm wrote that the capacity to be puzzled is important for creative development. Creative people don't turn and run at the first indication that the issue before them isn't black and white. I assert that you also need the readiness to be humble enough to ask questions. This open-mind attitude can be learned. Someone has described it as "constructive discontent." Most inventions came about because the inventor was dissatisfied with what was available. Don't resist being frustrated or puzzled when you face an old experience. Don't turn from it. Face and engage it in conversation.

What are some "worst times" people have? Consider the following unpleasant experiences: an unfair punishment or firing, being bullied in school, spending time in jail, getting caught in drug abuse, experiencing murder or rape in the family, having a child out of wedlock, premature death, domestic abuse or alcoholism, financial failure, racial or other kinds of discrimination, extreme poverty, a miscarriage, bankruptcy.

Think of positive experiences as well: an achievement of some kind from learning a new skill to learning a new language, being the first person in the family to graduate from college, climbing Mount Everest or achieving some other physical accomplishment, learning to walk after a long illness, overcoming fear of public speaking or traveling alone, receiving a promotion you had long awaited, recovering from a financial or natural disaster, giving birth, having a rare spiritual experience.

Once again, go through your grid (see page 28, Exercise 2) and list the best and worst times of each period. When you were a child, what made life wonderful? Mother's good food? Playing with friends in the empty lot and coming in late, dirty, and sweaty, but happy? What were your worst experiences as a child? Awareness you had been dishonest? Failing a grade?

When my daughter Christine was 17, she contracted lupus, an insidious auto-immune disease that mimics other disorders. After a near-death experience at the beginning of the summer, she and I began the long road to recovery so that she could begin college that fall. We traveled the long, arduous journey slowly, day by day, hour by hour. She had a few favorite records such as one by the Singing Nun, which we played by the hour.

That fall, she enrolled at the college where I was teaching. I recall my intense joy when I saw her slowly climb up the stairs in the administration building the first day of classes. Her courage to get well had paid off. It was a red-letter day for me, yet inside I wept to see her exertion. The struggle was not yet over. She won many battles over the next years, but not the war. She died 27 years later.

You know best what the worst and best times of your life were. Focus on one or two. They can be simple victories of the spirit, as well as great awards and diplomas. To write about yourself, you need the capacity to see yourself as a person separate from who you are now. Realize that if you lived through an experience, you probably can write about it now.

Folklore Improves the Flavor

The memory closets of all families hold a special kind of wealth, more valuable and interesting than the occasional skeleton that is dusted off for review at family reunions. These treasures include family stories, anecdotes, proverbs, humor, games, festivals, family expressions, customs, and traditions. Collecting family lore may take time but will reward you in many ways — first, by the good times you will have digging for it with other family members; and second, by the stacks of little treasures you can share with your readers that will tell them about the quality of your family life.

You may insert such material in your writing where appropriate, or you may want to make a chapter of it. As you collect it, be sure to identify where you found it and the date.

1. What is folklore?

The beliefs, stories, expressions and traditions of ordinary people that arise from the common life of ordinary people. It is any material that circulates traditionally among members of any group, usually in slightly different versions.

The little community where I grew up was superstitious, having its roots in European culture where ghosts had roamed the countryside for centuries. As children, we listened fearfully to ghost stories and stories about Satan, especially about a young man who sold his soul to the Devil. After the transaction, five strong men were needed to hold him down. He could literally climb walls. I heard the story again when I was at college in Winnipeg, Manitoba, and thereafter dismissed it until decades later when an aunt, living in Moscow, wrote me the story of her life telling the same story in great detail, and how the fear of the Devil ushered in a sweeping revival in her village of Friedenstal in the Ukraine. It brought about her conversion to Christianity. I included it in my compilation of family stories: *Into the Twilight Zone: Stories My Father Told Me Too Good to Throw Out* and gave the book to children one Christmas.

2. What are some of its characteristics?

It appears usually in the oral tradition, although today it travels by email, or by example. Within days, jokes about why the chicken crossed the road swept swiftly through cyberspace prior to the 2008 presidential election, with well-known political figures and celebrities giving an answer in keeping with their personality. A sister sent it to me from Canada. A friend read a series of answers at a luncheon.

Folklore is supposedly true and sometimes it is. The speaker begins with "Today I heard …", or "Last week someone told me …" A well-known legend that growing girls were reminded of in an earlier decade concerned a proud young woman who had her hair done in a bouffant style at the hairdressers and refused to comb it thoroughly for a week at a time. She died suddenly one day. The mortician found a black widow spider in her fancy hairdo. The moral was clear: Girls would suffer the same disaster if they didn't comb their hair thoroughly every day.

A folk story exists in various versions, always including certain details. The story about a boy who had never seen a woman until he was a young adult exists in Italian, German, and Jewish versions and possibly others with the same basic details. In the version my father brought from Russia, the father had taken the innocent boy into civilization where they chanced upon a group of young girls laughing at the street corner. The boy stood still and watched the girls with eyes getting ever bigger. "What are those creatures?" he asked his father. "Those are geese," said the father. "Oh, I like those geese," replied the boy.

Folk stories are usually anonymous without reliable documentation, yet the story about the young man selling his soul to the Devil is documented in a letter to me.

3. What are some types of folklore?

Stories and poems frequently arise from an ethnic or nationality group, a family, an occupational group, an age group, or a geographic area. The Jewish culture has spawned a large number of folk stories, many of them mocking themselves, possibly as a way of dealing with the hardships of persecution. Many ethnic groups can boast of a great many folk stories and customs, such as giving people nicknames to identify them more readily in communities where many people bear the same surname.

Food traditions are probably high on your list of folklore, especially if you derive from some ethnic group, but not necessarily. Nations such as the United States and Canada have their own traditions that differ from those of other countries. This difference becomes most apparent when you travel to another country or temporarily into another social class as my family did shortly after my husband died.

In 1962, one month after my husband died, an older couple from church took the children and me to dinner at a motel about 25 miles away from our home in Hillsboro, Kansas. Our family never ate in restaurants. Too expensive. We "enjoyed" a lot of liver, hot dogs, and similar food. Here at this restaurant, we encountered for the first time an American tradition—the all-you-can-eat buffet lunch. I wrote my parents:

> It was the sort of place where you can pick up what you like and eat as much of anything you want. I didn't ask for the amount of the bill! It must have been quite a size. Joanna was sure that our hosts were the wealthiest people in Hillsboro to afford such a meal. The food was simply delicious and there were about four different kinds of meat, dozens of relishes and pickles, etc. Of course, we tried nearly everything. It sure was wonderful and the children all behaved.

For many years thereafter when we received a phone call, "PB is cooking today. Would you join us for lunch on Sunday?" we knew it meant a trip to the buffet where the children could heap mashed potatoes on their plates and slather them with gravy, drink Coca-Cola to their hearts' content, and eat all the ice cream they wanted.

When traveling in Moscow in 1989, I was a little more urbanized with regard to eating other foods, but when my cousin Ellie placed a big bowl of something that looked like potato salad before me with perhaps a few extras, I said to myself, "This is going to be good." After I sat down, Eugene, her husband, poured a cup of *Kvass* (a mild ale) over it and Ellie added several tablespoons of sour cream. "Now stir it all together," she commanded. I stirred and prayed, "Lord, help me to eat this." It was remarkably good, for the Kvass is like a mild vinegar and the cream like oil.

One day in Halbstadt in the Molotschnaya, we bought some *Kvass* from a street vendor. The temperature was very warm and I needed a drink. The vendor merely briskly rinsed the glasses in a basin of murky water before reusing them for the next customer. To buy or not to buy? I bought. As the cool liquid trickled down, the memory of *Kvass* came back like a jolt of lightning. "I have drunk this before," I said to myself. Mother used to make *Kvass* out of fermented bread and sugar when we were children. She had brought the folk tradition along from the Ukraine.

Examine the food traditions in your family, your locality, and also in our country. They are an important part of your memoir writing.

With age as an established developmental stage, folk humor about this time of life has blossomed, sometimes to the extreme. I like to tell the story about the 70-ish woman who was well-educated, well-groomed, and yet dating a younger man. He was boorish, ill-kempt, and spoke without regard for word choice or syntax. Someone finally asked her why she wasted her time on such a person. Her answer came quickly. "He drives at night," she said. Young people for whom night driving holds no terrors can't understand why older adults with dimming eyesight and slower reflexes laugh uproariously at this joke.

Each geographic area produces its full quota of folklore. Kansas, where I live, has its share of stories related to tornadoes, snowstorms, droughts, grasshoppers, and ranching. What stories does your family have about the area you lived in?

Jokes, riddles, rhymes, tall tales, proverbs, or sayings are a large part of the folklore of some cultures. Some folk groups have a strong tradition of using proverbs to teach children, probably because their parents did the same with them. A gentle kind of folk wisdom was passed on through Low German sayings, which lose their original spice in translation. "If it tastes good, buy some for yourself" was said to someone watching you eat something particularly tasty. I grew up with "Many guests make an empty pantry," "Limitations reveal the master-worker," and "Sing before breakfast, cry before supper." If we nagged about when something would happen, the answer invariably was "next summer on Sunday three weeks later in the afternoon." My father had a traditional way of describing what today we might call casual clothing. He talked about wearing his "little-Sunday" clothes, a Low German phrase, which meant the clothes were not good enough for going to church, yet too good for work.

Memory of games such as Anthony over (Auntie-I-over), jacks, run my good sheep run, and dozens of others bring back related memories. The same is true for folk songs, ballads, dances, and lullabies. Common gestures, such as a thumbs up or down or sideways, time-out signals, and others are typical in today's culture. Here in America, we nod our heads if we agree. In India, I was perplexed because agreement was signaled by a sideways motion of the head.

4. **Why collect your family or other types of folklore?**
    a. Because it is an intriguing aspect of your background.
    b. It reveals how much various folk cultures have in common. Folk customs constantly absorb and reshape material from the past and from others.
    c. It shows how previous generations passed on wisdom or "lore."
    d. The stories make good conversational topics. They show very broadly people's concerns and fantasies over a period of time. Every family has special ways of using language for inside jokes that mean little to outsiders. Usually each family also has its store of tales about encounters with important personalities, children's misunderstandings of grown-up talk, as well as the odd tall tale or two.

Record a family story you heard growing up even though you may not think it is true. The following story is true.

> My father hated to hurt the feelings of even a cat. He believed admonition or criticism should be slipped into conversation sideways, never directly. One day he stood at the street corner leaning on the cane he used in his later decades and wearing heavy, dark glasses. Obviously, he looked perplexed to the young woman who asked if she could help him cross the street. Dad agreed and let her guide him by the arm across the street, never letting on he wasn't blind and could make it on his own.

Cherish your family stories and keep adding to them.

OPTIONAL
WRITING TASKS

How to Give Away What Can't
Be Counted or Measured

Life is much more than the sum of our collected stories. Most of us have much more to give away than things, yet our legal will only addresses the question: Who should get what when we die? Your legacy is much more than dollars and cents. In the literature about this topic, such writing is referred to as an "ethical will." Although I don't like the term, I'll use it to be consistent with other material on the subject.

Dr. Barry Baines, in *Ethical Wills: Putting Your Values on Paper*, states that you need time to reflect, the acceptance of your mortality, and the ability to write thoughts down clearly and succinctly in order to write an ethical will. Such wills have biblical precedents in Genesis 49, when the patriarch Jacob gathered his sons around his bed and gave each a specific blessing or curse. In Deuteronomy 33-34, Moses says farewell to the children of Israel. Baines writes there is evidence of such ethical wills in other cultures as well. At first it was done orally, and later on, when writing became common, this document was included with the person's last will and testament.

Susan Turnbull, author of *The Wealth of Your Life: A Step-by-Step Guide for Creating Your Ethical Will*, states that such a document will:

- Confirm what is important in your life and renew your appreciation of it.
- Create a personal message to those you love about what is priceless to you.
- Create a personal context for your material assets, such as why you are donating money to certain causes.
- Provide a personal explanation for possibly confusing aspects of your legal will.
- Link the past with future generations.
- Give you peace of mind because the most important things have been said.

Reflect at length about what you consider the worthwhile things about your life: values and virtues you cherished in your life, a specific story you don't want forgotten, specific teachings (religious, political, or moral) you cherish, or regrets in your life you would like your children to learn from. Don't forget your passions. What gave you joy in life? This is not bragging or boasting, but a declaration of the source of pleasure and meaning in your life. What are your hopes and wishes for children and grandchildren? What you have learned in life is as valuable as what you have in your bank account.

The design of your ethical will can take several formats: a letter addressed to your family generally, or specifically to each person; a lengthy essay; a video or audio message; a prayer for what you hope for your successors. This document could be read or given at the birth of a child, when children or grandchildren leave home, at retirement celebrations, anniversary or graduation events, family reunions, when facing a serious illness, or at the same time your legal will is read.

Here are two examples of letters I wrote, one to my granddaughter, Jamie, and the other to my great-nephew, Zachary, at their high school graduations.

Letter No.1 to a Granddaughter:

> Dear Jamie: Congratulations on finishing your high school education and being accepted at Northwestern University. May the coming years reward you richly in growth opportunities and lifelong friendships. For this you will need a lot of wisdom. How does one become wise? Here are a few tips I have learned along the way.

1. Wisdom doesn't always show up with age. Sometimes age shows up all by itself. Becoming one year older doesn't necessarily mean one year wiser.

2. Learn the difference between wisdom and knowledge. You can have one without the other. You can know a lot of facts about journalism, for example, but until you know how to apply them, they won't get you far. You can also be wise about life but know little or few facts about modern technology.

3. Some day soon you will be a sophomore at North-western, but don't remain a sophomore all your life in attitudes. The word "sophomore" comes from the Greek roots for "wisdom" (*sophos*) and "moron." A sophomore is a moron who thinks she's wise. Don't stay in that stage. Keep growing as a person.

4. "The fear of the Lord is the beginning of wisdom." But remember also, "The fool has said in his heart there is no God." For me, my faith in God is non-negotiable.

5. Deliberately find a mentor in an older woman, maybe 10 to 20 years older than you are, at all times of your life, to encourage, advise, and love you. I have done this for decades, and, as one woman died, I found another. Even at my age, I need a mentor to guide me through these decades of growing older.

6. Wisdom is knowing when to say, "It's time to quit this and try another tactic." Don't be too proud to admit you made a wrong choice.

7. Wisdom is knowing when to say, "I'm sorry. Forgive me."

8. Wisdom is also knowing when to forgive someone – your roommate, for example, who may have offended you – without being asked to do so. By being unforgiving, you may feel you are in control, but the opposite is true. So forgive. And don't sweat the small stuff.

9. Don't hesitate to risk in learning to know new people who don't fit into your prescribed categories for people worth knowing, such as race, social background, age, and education. I don't think I need to include gender!

10. Wisdom is always respecting and loving your family of origin. I was once ashamed of my immigrant background, but eventually found out that my real riches lay in my German–Russian heritage. I love you, Jamie. Have a great year.

– *Grandma Katie*

Letter No. 2 to a Great-Nephew:

Dear Zachary: Congratulations on finishing high school and being accepted at a university for more studies. I want to tell you something about faithfulness and keeping promises, the key to successful living.

My father, Jacob J. Funk, was a storekeeper in a small rural village in northern Saskatchewan. Customers charged groceries, sometimes for six to nine months, and then when the harvest came in September or October, they paid their bills. But sometimes they weren't faithful or true to their earlier promise to pay, and went to another store when they couldn't face Dad. As you move into life, how can you make your promises an integral part of your character?

1. Your promise has the power to create and determine your future. A promise to be a soccer player means taking yourself off the sidelines and committing yourself to playing the game. An uncommitted player isn't worth much. And an uncommitted student isn't worth much to himself or to the school. So be committed to this new venture.

I remember two brothers from the days before student loans and scholarships. Both brothers wanted to be doctors, so the younger brother, Jake, offered to work at common labor and put his brother, Abe, through medical school. What if the older brother had said on graduation, "Forget what we agreed to before I went to med school. I now have a family to provide for"? Faithfulness to a promise was at the heart of that agreement. Both brothers became doctors. Their promises created their future.

2. When you make a promise to someone, you are exercising your free will. A true promise to remain faithful is never forced on you. When I was young, when we went to work we were committed to putting in five eight-hour days of work each week. That was our promise when we

were hired. In whatever vocation you choose, always be faithful in giving your supervisors your full commitment and energy. This is your choice. Only free people can make promises. A slave or prisoner can't promise to work for someone else next week.

3. The degree of your faithfulness, or the way you keep your promises, establishes your identity. When I was teaching at Tabor College in Hillsboro, Kansas, I got requests from prospective employers for student evaluations. As a student, you may think your main identity comes from your academic achievements and extracurricular successes, but I believe it comes even more from the way you keep your promise to attend class, get assignments done, and do your own work. When you break a promise, you betray yourself and also disappoint others. And people remember those broken promises. Faithfulness is the real measure of a man. You have my best wishes for the years ahead.

– *Your Great-Aunt Katie Funk Wiebe*

WRITING OPTION:

Write an essay or letter to some relative or friend in which you give away those things you treasure that can't be counted, measured, weighed, or handled.

In *The Dead Beat: Lucky Stiffs and the Perverse Pleasures of Obituaries,* which is about the art, history, and subculture of obituary writings, Marilyn Johnson writes that we are living in the golden age of such writing. The flowery prose of obituary writing of the 19th century changed to perfunctory prose, and then about 25 years ago, there was another huge shift. Whereas at one time only the rich and famous were privileged to have well-written obituaries, newspapers discovered that the extraordinary in the ordinary person's life could profoundly move the reader. And so the modern obituary that moved beyond bare facts to the real life of the person was born. The obituary page is often the most read (or at least most scanned) page of the newspaper.

A reviewer of Johnson's *The Dead Beat* makes the case that the superior obituary is far more than the announcement of a death and a recitation of the highlights of a person's life. Well-written obituaries tell "the uniqueness of each life lived and what is now lost forever and irredeemably. . . . They are literary instruments capable of verve, insight, empathy, historical resonance, and humor." And, believe it or not, today there is even A Great Obituary Writers International Conference with competitions for the best obituary.

Write that best obituary for yourself. Such sketches are helpful to survivors, for they might not remember specific dates of birth, employment, or retirement. They might not know proper spellings of people's names, places, companies, or organizations. Even more, they might not fully grasp the intensity of your life passions if they lived at a distance. In a self-written obituary you can specify a favorite charity for donations that your family may not have thought of. What slant do you want to give to your life? When you write your own life sketch, you can include humor or pathos, or both.

Consider also writing your own *epitaph* for your cemetery marker. If you don't, someone will put your name and dates on the gravestone and add "dearly beloved or maybe something worse," says one writer. An epitaph is your last chance to communicate something to the world. Mobster Al Capone chose these words: "My Jesus, mercy." Take every opportunity to speak to an audience of any kind.

What should you include in your life summary?

- Full legal name and nicknames if you had any. Why you were called a nickname would be interesting.
- Date of birth, where you were born and to whom. Add any little details related to this birth, if you know them.
- Main cities or towns of residence
- Marriage and children
- Education
- Work record
- Associations
- Awards
- Volunteer work
- Hobbies
- Military service

- Travel
- Family members, with full names and the relationship of deceased and living relatives

But is this enough? I don't think so. What were the little things about your life that made it interesting? What will be missing from people's lives when you are gone? Who will miss you besides your cat? What was the passion of your life? This is particularly important. Was it golf? Or was it cleaning the silverware? Maybe it was a zeal to help an underprivileged child. Or maybe you were a secret poet. Don't let your humility get in the way of your writing.

WRITING OPTION:

Write a summary sketch of your entire life. In this sketch you want to include the main facts and highlights of your life. It should show that you lived and didn't just move from date to date. It could be used later on as the basis for an obituary. It will help you focus on the wholeness of your life, not just the bits and pieces. Barring major disasters, life is rarely lived in isolated incidents, but moves from one event to another.

FINAL HURDLES TO THE FINISHED PRODUCT

Hurdle No. 1: The Temptation to Quit

Some people start a project with great enthusiasm and then quit, cold turkey, because they face a hurdle. They think they can't jump. They shelve everything, sometimes never picking up their writing again. From my years of teaching memoir writing classes, I find these are usually the reasons:

1. **"I don't have anything to say. My life wasn't very interesting."**
Remind yourself again that zestful living is not restricted to other people's families. Good things, interesting things, happen regularly and

often in the lives of mothers and fathers, neighbors, teachers – ordinary people. They happen in your life. Dig for them until you find them.

You have lived 24 hours every day for the last 70 or 80 years. Something was always happening. Write about the little things of life, such as how you saved money one summer to buy a bike, or how you watched a withdrawn child move toward other people. Look at the small moments, rather than hoping to come upon big, earth-shaking events. Begin small with short stories, and keep adding to them. Write more about less.

My sister, Sue, and I have been trying to piece together a story that probably happened when I was about 14. I call it "The Saga of the Rhinestone Necklace."

One fall, toward the end of the Depression, an unusual family moved into our little village. The husband was white, the wife was white, but the two older children were black and the youngest was white. Gossip said the Welshes had circus connections.

That winter, my friend Mona and I, in a sudden fit of missionary zeal, visited their home late one afternoon. Evening in that far northern area comes early, so the little hovel was dimly lit, the atmosphere uninviting. I recall seeing a single loaf of bread dough rising on the stove warmer, looking as if it could sit there all day like a lump of clay and never rise. We left quickly. Our zeal also quickly faded in the face of such stark poverty.

> In spring, before the family moved from our community, Mrs. Welsh, a tiny, tired-looking woman in washed-out clothing, came to my father in the store and pressed a rhinestone necklace into his hands as her thanks for the food he had given them during the winter. I am always uncovering more evidence of my father's generosity to the poor.

In 1966, when I was beginning freelance writing, I returned from a writers' conference in Wisconsin with new ideas and zeal. Editors kept saying they were looking for material with a seasonal emphasis. I had just had a story (based on the facts above) rejected by Canada's nationwide *Family Herald and Weekly Star*, which featured a black family like the Welshes in my childhood village, living in a white community in northern Saskatchewan. So I changed the time of the story to late fall, and added a Christmas school concert. I called the story "The Red Catalogue Dress," in which a little black girl and a rich doctor's daughter both wear the same Eaton's catalogue red velvet dress to the concert, leading to a surprise ending. I sent it off to the *Family Herald* once again. In two weeks, I received a check for $125.

But here the actual story gets even more interesting. At some point, my father gave the rhinestone necklace to my oldest sister, who years later gave it to a niece, who in the spring of 2008 gave it to her daughter, Olivia, to wear to her prom. Was this necklace once worn by a circus performer? Are there more pieces to this puzzle?

If you tell a meaningful story, people will be interested. The challenge is to identify those experiences that have meaning beyond your life. Aim for reader interest rather than sounding important. Write, write, and write. Find a bigger wastepaper basket if need be, but keep writing.

2. "I don't have time to write."

Until you see writing your life story as a task that must be done, like watering the lawn, shopping for groceries, and brushing your teeth, you won't have time. Look at your calendar and put writing on it for a few hours several times a week, and then don't let other engagements take over. Protect this time as carefully as attending the birthday party of a grandchild. This writing time also belongs to your children and grandchildren.

3. "I don't feel inspired."

If you wait for inspiration to show up first, you will never write. Madeleine L'Engle, author of *A Wrinkle in Time*, asserts that "writing a book is work; it involves discipline, and writing when I don't feel like writing. Robert Louis Stevenson said that writing is 10 percent inspiration, and 90 percent perspiration. The inspiration doesn't come before the perspiration. … Inspiration comes during work, not before it." More than one class member has told me that the more she became involved in her writing project, the more inspired she became to continue.

4. "I don't know how to organize all the stuff I've gathered."

You have pages of writing, files full of research. Now what? The best approach is to sit back and look at everything you have pulled together as if from a distance. When you're too close, all you see is individual trees. From a distance, you will begin to see clumps of trees here, flowers over there, and a pond in another direction. Go back to the original grid (see page 28, Exercise 2) and review it several times until you see a pattern evolving. Sort similar ideas together first in a paragraph or two, then in a chapter. Don't hesitate to cut and paste. Computers are wonderful for that task.

5. "I don't know who to write for."

A common audience for the kind of writing we are aiming for is family and close friends. If you don't have a family, set your sights on a general audience of peer adults. If you are writing for children, your subject matter, tone, and language use will have to shift to their level. Knowing your audience and keeping it in mind all the time is the key to successful writing.

6. "I feel uncomfortable writing from the first-person viewpoint."

As I've already said, years ago using "I" in writing was a big taboo. Teachers hammered this into students so much that today we have people saying "Johnny and me are going to a party," assuming that to stick an "I" into a sentence is a big no-no. Don't assume you can write about yourself without sticking yourself in the middle of the action. Otherwise, the result is usually something blah and boring.

First person is best for an autobiography. Don't let the reader lose sight of you. You are the main character of your story. The reader wants stories that will reveal you as a person who occasionally lost your temper when you were out of sorts or forgot to take out the trash. This is difficult for some people. They dislike revealing what they think or how they felt, men more than women. As William Zinsser writes in *On Writing Well*, at least think "I" while you write.

You may share a recipe or a joke in a letter to a friend or relative, but you would omit this in correspondence to the mortgage company explaining why you are late with a payment. By labeling something a life story or history, you are promising your readers this is not going to be only facts about the Depression or the turbulent '60s, but about how you were involved and affected by these periods. Readers want to see you as a human being, so use "I" and "me" and "we" and "us" as required.

The trend is shifting to using "you" instead of "one" as the impersonal pronoun. "One should not stay in the bathtub for more than four hours at a time" inspires the flippant reader to say, "OK, but should two do it?" Use "you" instead of "one" in informal prose.

First-person plural (we) is awkward in telling a story. It immediately removes the story one step away from the main character. Even if you are writing about married life, keep it your story. Talk about "my husband and I" rather than "we thought, we felt, we wanted to do this." Husband and wives are not clones, so don't profess to always know what your spouse was thinking. Compare "we all felt she was too bold in her pronouncements" with "I felt she was too bold. My husband said he agreed with me."

Third person (he, she) is sometimes evasive when used to refer to yourself. Choose one point of view and stick to it, with some leeway, of course.

Write to find the truth about yourself. Aim to be authentic, true to your experience. Insincere writing is easily identified. You are an authority on your own life, so write confidently. Own your life. It's yours to give away, so don't hesitate to say, "I trembled when I ...."

7. "I can't decide what to include and what to leave out."

Autobiographers tend to include too much and biographers too little. Annie Dillard writes in her memoir, *An American Childhood,* that she leaves out many important things that have no concern for the present book she is writing. She doesn't take readers on a wonderful summer trip to Wyoming if she is telling a story about something that happened in Pittsburgh. She leaves out her involvement with various young men. She leaves out anything that might trouble the family. She leaves out her grievances about life. These are your decisions to make. Leave out whatever doesn't fit your theme. Save that for another book.

8. "I don't know if something happened the way I remember it. My brother says it happened differently."

When faced with conflicting views of an event, use the source closest to the event at the time. Use the source most capable of understanding and describing the situation as it happened. A burglary occurs in your neighbor's home. Present were a four-year-old and his mother. Whose account is more believable?

Find motivation for an event. After the Russian Revolution, my father, newly married, undertook a lengthy journey on foot through war-ravaged areas to find my mother's family, lost during the upheaval. He was at risk of being murdered any time for the few crusts in his knapsack. He kept at his mission until he found Mother's parents and seven siblings in a hovel far from their home, which had been razed during the fighting. Motivation for his arduous journey concerned me for a long time. As I studied his life more closely, I found that motivation in his character and could write the story, published in *The Storekeeper's Daughter*.

I had two versions of another story I wanted to include in one of my books told from the standpoints of my father, at about age 25, and his youngest brother, who was 12 or 13 at the time. I decided to go with his younger brother's version because he was closer to the event at the time and probably remembered better the emotional event of having his father lined up against the wall to be shot as a political prisoner. My father heard the story secondhand.

Remember, these are your memories. Your goal is to share your life rather than to set the record straight.

Writing Tip:

Keep your own views separate in your notes from those of your sources. I often simply write "Katie" – and then my own thoughts so that I don't have my subject saying what I thought. I learned that in graduate school as I took lecture notes. One side of the page was for lecture notes, the other side for my response to what was being said.

9. "What do I do if I can't remember?"

You're at a dead end. Go back and do some of the beginning exercises again (grid, floor plan, timeline). If you really can't remember, let it go or mention it briefly. Don't make it up. Use your subconscious mind. This is not something mystical or magical. Often if you ponder a problem at length one day, then let go of it, the next morning you may find the solution has come. Most problem-solvers use this method.

10. "How do I keep from vilifying people (and even myself) or making them too holy (hagiography)?"

Aim for objectivity when writing about something that is very emotional to you. To write romantically, defensively, or sentimentally about an experience without an honest appraisal of the contrast between the incident and the real world doesn't ring true.

Keep a balance between the negative and positive. Don't exploit the past to lift yourself up. It may not make as good a story, but it will be more authentic and true. To dramatize too much can be as dangerous as too much sensational openness. To blow up a story too much is as dangerous as too much reticence. Aim for meaning, not for a moral or a sermon. Avoid preaching and moralizing even if you were a preacher. Readers always have their radar out to detect phoniness or too much schmaltz.

Avoid adverbs and adjectives in the superlative degree to describe people. "My uncle was the most wonderful gardener in the whole world" is overblown. That statement would be difficult to prove. A fundamental in using adjectives and adverbs is not to let one of them smother the effect of another strong word. "Don't let your straight man steal the attention from the comic," states Ken Macrorie in *Telling Writing*. If you write, "she was unusually hideous," you have lessened the force of "hideous" by making the reader attend to the weak word "unusually." Your writing will be stronger if you avoid words like "so," "very," "tremendously," and so forth.

11. "I have changed my mind about attitudes and values I held earlier."

It is hard to record harsh opinions held long ago, such as my elitist attitude toward the African-American children in my story. I also recall when I severely judged mothers who worked outside the home or hired babysitters so they could enjoy time away from their children. When circumstances forced me to work outside the home to earn a living for my family, my opinions had to change or I couldn't live with myself. We interpret the past in light of the present and the present in light of the past. If things are going well now, the present can overpower the past and possibly negate earlier attitudes. Memories of a good past also can deceive us about our true feelings if life is rough now.

It is better to say "I changed my mind" about racism, for example, than to pretend your current feelings dropped out of the sky full-blown or to deny that once you were a strong supporter of white supremacy. Admit to being a racist, if that was the case, but then trace how your attitude changed. To help you, make a list of all the things you have changed your mind about. Memoirs are about change, not about staying the same.

12. "I don't know whether to name people by their right names."

You can make a disclaimer at the beginning of the book that all characters' names have been changed. But why shouldn't you name your siblings or friends and relatives? Will it hurt anyone if you do?

Watch the use of relational terms like "Mother" or "Mama" to refer to various people in the same writing. In former days, many husbands called their wives, "Mama," especially in front of the children. You can get yourself into a tangled situation when you introduce your husband's mother, whom he calls "Mama," and then your own mother, also called "Mama," and then have your husband and your children also calling you "Mama." When you start writing, make clear how you are going to refer to your relatives, whether by a relational term or given name.

13. **"I don't know what to do about difficult experiences such as drug and alcohol abuse, divorce, domestic violence, prejudice, fighting in the home, unfaithfulness, incest."**

Some stories are hard to write about because they may embarrass other family members or cause hard feelings. There is the danger of turning your memoir into a confessional of inner thoughts and outward actions to get attention, or to get even. You will find yourself wanting to edge away from the truth. Don't avoid only lies; also avoid half-truths that lead to the wrong impression. No one can force you to tell something you want to keep under cover.

Clarify your motives first. Avoid libel. Avoid hurting unnecessarily. Ask yourself why you want to include a certain event. Is it for malice, spite, to be sensational, to set the record straight, to debunk, to let people know how unfairly you were treated? Then ask what purpose it will accomplish if you include it. Has the matter been resolved? Is it fair to all concerned? Will it build goodwill and better family relationships in the future?

While copy-editing a book of religious conversion stories, I noticed that some writers were explicit in describing early misbehaviors. Did they really want a full description of their youthful indiscretions on record for children and grandchildren to read? I brought this to the attention of the editor, who modified some stories. It is possible to mention some actions without necessarily going into scintillating detail to make the writing more titillating.

What new perspective has time brought to the issue? Recognize that age, social status, theology, attitudes, and reputation in society will influence how you view discarded emotions, beliefs, and causes you once staunchly supported. If the unpleasant event happened when you were well in control of your life, you usually will continue to view it with acceptance. If you are unhappy now, you will tend to blame the past and view it in a darker light. The power of the past to continue to control or deceive remains strong. You may have dropped out of high school because of a domineering teacher, but age has shown you that your own attitude toward learning, coupled with an unhappy home life, was as much to blame.

Talk to people if necessary and get releases. How much did the experience affect you? Does it further your story or will it take people down a side path? In Maya Angelou's *I Know Why the Caged Bird Sings*, she tells how her mother's boyfriend tried to rape her. That event is integral to her story because it resulted in her loss of speech for some time until a teacher helped her overcome her fears.

Emphasize the event rather than the people involved. In the Old Testament book of Genesis, the story about Joseph meeting his brothers emphasizes the act of his betrayal as a child rather than the betrayers. Joseph says, "I am Joseph. Does my father yet live? Do not grieve, for God sent me before you to preserve life," rather than "You, my brothers, are to blame for the sorry mess you are in."

Omitting the difficult experience may be an option to consider. Recognize it as your problem to deal with, not someone else's, unless it is something that openly involved many other people. Avoid using your children's stories to make your story more exciting. Tell your story and let them tell theirs.

14. **"How do I handle major successes and victories?**
    What about failures, disappointments, regrets,
    and lessons I have learned?"

Be as objective as possible. You can mention major successes without gloating. A friend kept begging me to write his biography. "Why don't you do it yourself?" I asked him. "If I wrote it, I couldn't boast about myself like another person could," he said. Ups and downs show you are a real person, not a cardboard figure. If the story of your faith life shows only miraculous answers to prayer, one after another, each more astounding and amazing than the other, people will think you belong in heaven already, not here where most of us struggle with trials and failures. Simply offer yourself as an example of the process of living.

Hurdle No. 2: Making Your Writing More Readable and Interesting

Writing and speaking are not the same. Most people don't speak the way they write and don't write the way they speak. They shift gears completely, speaking understandably to a friend but writing in almost another language.

Writing and speaking are dialects of the same language. When you speak, your audience has the benefit of gestures, inflections, and facial expressions. When you write, you have to create emphasis and special meanings with your word choice, punctuation, and word arrangement.

Don't attempt emphasis by using all capital letters or a half dozen exclamation marks or inserting "SO" in boldface after every other phrase like confetti at a wedding to let the reader know you mean what you say. Toss words like "wow" into your mental wastebasket.

Writing that sounds as if it is being spoken but has been crafted to achieve that effect without the verbosity of spoken language is most effective. This book is being written as if I have you sitting in front of me. How would my tone change if I used "the writer" instead of "I" and "one" instead of "you" for the impersonal pronoun?

The characteristics of reader-based prose are *clarity, precision, and concision.* I like to add a fourth item to this traditional trio: *interesting.* I dislike reading dull material. I also don't like to read and reread material to figure out the meaning. I've only got so much time, so I advise you not to clothe a wisp of an idea in a 350-pound man's pajamas.

The study of readability was a popular area of journalism research in the 1960s and '70s. The experiments made by Rudolf Flesch and Robert Gunning revealed that much written material was simply not easy enough for most people to understand. Today, communication experts use readability tests on a piece of writing intended for the public. Examine the following samples I used in my college teaching and decide which are more readable – by simply glancing at them.

Sample 1:

> The chemical age gives every highly technical nation
> a choice between self-sufficiency and trade on whatever

barter or bargaining basis it desires, thus upsetting time-honored geographical alignments of monopolies of certain natural products and altering the whole concept of imperialism. This is an entirely new situation for agriculture. For centuries the threat of eventual scarcity of food and land hung over the world. Within a few decades the march of science has brought about a compete reversal. On the one hand, the chemist and the technologist have made possible the production of greater and greater quantities of products on less and less land, resulting in enormous surpluses of acreage, crops, and labor. At the same time, ironically enough, the chemist is removing one product after another from the soil into the laboratory, throwing still more land out of cultivation and further reducing the amount of labor needed.

Sample 2:

A good will is good not because of what it performs or effects, not by its aptness for the attainment of some proposed end, but simply by virtue of the volition, that is, it is good in itself, and considered by itself to be esteemed much higher than all that can be brought about by it in favor of any inclination, nay, even of the sum total of all inclinations. Even if it should happen that, owing to special disfavor of fortune, or the stingy provision of a step–motherly nature, this will should wholly lack power to accomplish its purpose ....

Sample 3:

"Cheer up, sir," said Mrs. Crupp. "I can't bear to see you so, sir. I'm a mother myself."

I did not quite perceive the application of this fact to myself, but smiled on Mrs. Crupp, as benignly as was in my power.

"Come, sir," said Mrs. Crupp. "Excuse me. I know that it is, sir. There's a lady in the case."

"Mrs. Crupp?" I returned, reddening.

"Oh, bless you. Keep a good heart, sir!" said Mrs. Crupp, nodding encouragement. "Never say die, sir. If she don't smile upon you, there's a many as will. You are a young gentleman."

Given a choice, which of the three samples looks more readable? Why? It has to do with length of average sentences, number of words in sentences and white space. Little children begin reading with two- to six-word sentences. Post-graduate students are expected to read sentences with up to 240 words. The number of syllables in words also affects readability. Notice that Sample 3 has mostly one- and two-syllable words, even though it was written for adults. Adult reading does not have to be incomprehensible to be considered good writing.

Another determining factor in readability is the percentage of words and sentences with human interest, which Flesch and Gunning label "personal words." Such words include names of people or animals, personal pronouns, and words that deal with human beings or their relationships (man, woman, boy, girl, father, son, aunt). Count the number of personal words in each of the above three samples.

An additional factor in readability is your diction or choice of words. At times I get homesick for language used carefully, lovingly, decisively. I catch myself *tsk-tsk*-ing speakers who are word-poor and hiccup words like "just" and "like" after every few phrases and lack any adjectives other than "nice," "great," and "awesome." Some resort to vulgarisms and obscenities to express strong emotion.

You become a more honest writer when you move close to the idea, object, experience, or person you want to write about. When you see the details with all your senses, you can choose descriptive words more carefully. Here are a few general principles about diction:

1. Prefer the specific word to the general whenever you can. Too much generalization leads to an impersonal tone in your writing. General words refer to a class or name a whole group of things. They say less and less about more and more. Specific words are the close-up words. They name members of a class. "Vegetables" is a general word, "carrots" a specific one.

Examine this paragraph by a college freshman and note the lack of specific words:

It is really exciting to learn to run your own life in a responsible way. Second, it is interesting to learn to know so many new kids from so many new places. There are kids from many different backgrounds with many different ideas gathered in one place, and the freshmen have the privilege of being part of this varied group and also learn- ing from this group of people. I think the freshmen have a slight advantage because we are not yet set in our college routine and will probably be more open-minded.

2.   Always support an abstraction with concrete examples. Concrete words convey "thing-ness" or concreteness. By "concrete" I mean tangible things we can touch, taste, feel, see, or measure. A concrete word brings an image to mind. When I say axe, book, wastepaper basket, mouse, or rain, an image comes to mind immediately.

Abstract words cannot be pictured clearly. Try creating an image of love, friendship, loneliness, and patriotism. Immediately you are forced to bring the abstract to the level of the concrete. Abstract words refer to the qualities of tangible things. They have no exact combination of physical properties to which the reader can refer. Abstract words do not zero in. They can mean anything. New writers migrate toward them because they're popular, quick to find, and easy to use.

Example: Oh, I was so blessed. She was beautiful.

Neither statement conveys a clear image, only vague emotions. One way to check the power of an abstraction is by forcibly reuniting abstract words with particular concrete details.

Happiness is a warm puppy.

Hope is checking your e-mail every hour.

Innocence is …

Misery is …

3. Always choosing the precisely right word with the connotation you intend makes your writing richer. What abstract idea (emotion) is my daughter Christine trying to convey about her experience waiting beside her sister about to give birth at home?

ECLIPSE

My hands are ready, sister,

waiting to touch the dark diamond of his crown,

a rim of white skin.

All this womb-wrapped night I wait beside you.

Your kneeling frame swells,

fingers clench wood.

Damp, black elfin head fills my palms.

Shaking, I grasp warm, wet shoulders,

Blinded by light from the other side of the moon.

– *Christine R. Wiebe*

Hurdle No. 3: Revising and Polishing

George Bernard Shaw sent early drafts of his plays to his friend Ellen Terry, the actress, for criticism. She said she feared to suggest changes to his manuscript.

He wrote back: "Oh, bother the [manuscripts], mark them as much as you like. What else are they for? Mark everything that strikes you. I may consider a thing 49 times, but if you consider it, it will be considered 50 times; and a line 50 times considered is two percent better than a line 49 times considered. And it is the final two percent that makes the difference between excellence and mediocrity."

As you revise your work, look for these common weaknesses in your writing, especially wordiness, the bane of beginning writers. Less is usually more. Wordiness also is referred to as deadwood, verbiage, or jargon. A weak, wordy sentence will usually have these features:

1. Excessive use of all forms of the verb "to be," as in "it is (was)" and "there is (was)". The verb "is" is a weak verb; all it does is link, not show action. In its class are also "to be, go, get, have, come, try, and began to, start to, seem, etc."

   By a poll it was revealed that ...

   It was a beautiful spring day when we went ...

   There were about twenty people attending the meeting.

   It seems that of the both groups, the boys are more conscious than the girls about the niceties of dress. Edited: Boys are more clothes-conscious than girls.

2.   Excessive use of passive verbs (doer of the action is not in subject position). A story doesn't begin until the main character is introduced, if only with a pronoun. A sentence doesn't begin to convey meaning until the true subject is introduced. In the passive voice, the receiver of the action shows up in subject position. The doer of the action (true subject) is omitted or placed in a "by" phrase.

I like to compare the passive voice to long underwear getting tangled in the washing machine with other items like bra straps and apron strings. Prefer the active voice unless there is good reason to use the passive. Using the passive is a bad habit to get into, like chewing gum in public. You do it because you've always done so. Heavy use of the passive results in a slow, pedantic style. What is the true subject (doer of the action) in these sentences?

The dog was clawed by the cat.

The scheme was conceived by John at four in the morning.

The play was observed by Mary with amazing indifference.

Who gave the order in this sentence? Omitting the true subject lets the writer off the hook in identifying him or herself, which is the reason it is often used by people in authority.

The order was given to all students to come earlier on Friday.

There are two passives in this sentence. Can you identify them?

It must be remembered that the Apostle Paul's thinking was shaped by his Hebrew background.

3. Excessive use of adjectives and adverbs slows the reader and muddies the meaning.

> *Between the intellectual silences was a zealous sigh of exasperation coming from the aggressive letter reader. Without further ado he withdrew from the premises to his own place of secure refuge and we went on continuing our laborious endeavors of the mind's learning process.*

4. Your writing is stronger without the unnecessary use of intensifying words like "tremendously," and "great, big, very, so, really, etc."

> *She was so hideous.*
> *She was very unhappy about the new arrival.*

5. Substituting a strong expression to make up for a weak opinion makes your writing weaker: "indeed, obviously, of course, surely, certainly, needless to say, honestly, frankly sincerely, in fact."

> *We certainly want you to come.*
> *I sincerely hope you will be with us tonight.*

6. Introducing apologetic words to soften your views also weakens writing.

> *It was sort of a flop.*
> *He was kind of a hero to me.*
> *That, incidentally, is four fouls.*
> *Falling down the stairs isn't too useful.*

7.   Omitting antecedents for pronouns, or unclear use of pronouns, especially "this" and "it."

Some of the classes were combined and met in the same room. This irritated the teacher.

8.   Use of trite expressions such as "nice, pretty, awful, big, fantastic, fine, great, like, lovely, marvelous," and dozens more. These words, called "utility" words, lead to vagueness. I've heard them referred to also as bargain, counter, or even "weasel" words that sneak into writing and weaken it. They are a dime for two dozen. Any word that doesn't lend itself to measurement fits this category.

The problem with this kind of treasure is that it is all too perishable.

We weren't too happy because the motel looked rather cheap.
He was so delighted to receive the award.

9.   Using awkward repetition before examples.

The novel was outstanding for several reasons. One reason it was outstanding is that everything had a meaning and a place.

10.   Using nonessential phrases.

<u>I would like to say that I believe</u> television could be an effective educational medium.

Henry Clay <u>was an</u> intelligent and vital <u>type of person</u>.
<u>It all happened</u> on a bright sunny day in June.
<u>There are often</u> many people involved in such volunteer work.

11.   Overweight nouns, especially long Latinate ones with endings like -tion, -ment and -ence. Take time to count the number of four- or more syllable words in your work.

The first area of language translation is authority. Translationists like secularization's dethroning of traditional authorities. Translationists are comfortable with critical probing of the original text or other authorities. They accept critical scholarship, which uses, as the foundation for studying all authorities, the one authority secularization allows as their critical, scientific methodology.

A crisis of degradation is enveloping the earth. (Does a crisis envelop?)

Local weather forecaster: Sedgwick County is experiencing thunderstorm activity. (Isn't a thunderstorm an activity?)

12.   Use of the pronoun "we" without making clear who "we" is. When the nurse asked my daughter in the hospital, "Shall we have our bath now?" she would respond: "I don't know what you want to do, but I'd like a bath."

13.   English is a word order language, not an inflectional one. Usual order: Subject–Verb-Object/complement. In English, the subject and verb should be as close together as possible. When you break the word order, you are ungrammatical.

We went to the movies yesterday. (grammatical)

We went yesterday to the store. (ungrammatical)

Hurdle No. 4: Publishing

Although you may not have finished writing, it is wise to start thinking what you will do with your story when you have typed the last word. What are the next steps?

1. Go over your manuscript one last time to make sure you have said what you intended to say. Once it is in print, you can't take it back. Your aim is to entertain, to inform, to offer yourself as an example of the human process. You are concerned with shaping, with making sense out of the past from the standpoint of the present. Therefore, your life story will never be the whole story, only part of it. Take another look at form, order, clarity of ideas. Double-check all names, dates, and statements of fact.

    Have someone else read it for grammar, spelling, punctuation, sentence structure, consistency of style, and wordiness. Never let your only copy of your manuscript leave your possession. Be sure to have at least one or more copies. If you work on a computer, make a copy on an external drive. The other person may lose it through negligence, fire, or tornado.

2. If you decide on an alternative method of publishing, know your options. This decision is answered by the audience you wrote your book for, the size of that audience, and the funds available to you for publishing. Talk to people who have had their memoirs

published and ask what they learned from the experience. Here is a brief review of the possibilities.

Commercial royalty publisher. This means you market your manuscript to a commercial publisher, who contracts to buy the manuscript, publish, and market it and give you a return on the sales. Publishers need to be certain they will sell enough books to make a profit on the contract. They take full responsibility for editing, publishing, publicizing, storing inventory, and selling the books. Once you have signed the contract, the manuscript belongs to them until both of you make another arrangement on its ownership. You give up editorial control, including choice of title, cover design, and other details.

Vanity publisher. Stay away from such publishers. They appeal to the creators' vanity and desire to become a published author. They make their money from fees charged to the creator of the work for their services rather than from sales of published material to retailers and consumers. Such publishers sometimes disguise themselves as "subsidy publishers." The vanity publisher offers some fringe benefits such as editing, design, warehousing, advertising, and distribution for a fee for such services. The author takes all the risk and pays all the cost of publication, marketing, storage, and so forth.

Bookstores and libraries are usually wary of vanity publishers. Vanity publishers have the reputation for being exploitive in that they praise manuscripts beyond their true worth, so that new writers are led to believe they have a product that will make them rich. They push you to buy many more copies than you need, so you may end up with a garage full of books.

Subsidy or joint publisher, sometimes confused with vanity publisher. Watch whatever you sign. Such publishers accept manuscripts they think meet their editorial policy and ask for a subsidy from the author to assist in publishing. You let go of control of your manuscript, the same as with a royalty publisher.

Print on demand (POD). Once you have a single clean copy, you can turn to POD publishers to print as few or as many as you want, within a few days sometimes.

Publishing your manuscript on your own Web site and allowing readers to download it for themselves. My brother, Jack Funk, published the second edition of his book *Outside the Women Cried* online. Google the title or his name.

Self-publisher. You may do best to follow the example of an elderly woman who had completed her memoirs. A vanity publisher offered to publish her book for $6,000. Friends advised her to wait for a royalty publisher because she had such an interesting life. Her answer to them was "I'm 83, you know. I've been through the '20s and the '30s. I want to leave a book behind, but the publishers say they have hundreds of the kind I have written. They take six months to answer a letter. Waiting is fine if you live to be 150." She published her memoirs herself. I advise you to do the same.

As a self-publisher, you have control of the entire process of editing and publishing, as well as storing inventory and marketing. You recognize that your manuscript is of no interest to a commercial publisher. Making money is not the object. Often self-publishers market directly to their target audience or even give the books away. As creator of your work you retain editorial control of the content, arranging for printing, marketing the material, and distributing it to consumers or to retailers. The financial risk is entirely yours.

Have someone type your manuscript on a computer using desktop publishing software. Decide whether to include photos, charts, or drawings. Get some help planning the cover. **Proofread the manuscript again**. And again. Choose a compelling title for each chapter as well as the book. Then have the manuscript in print-ready form duplicated by a commercial photocopying service. The same business will bind it for you using either saddle stitch, coil, comb, side stitch, square binding or hardback. Take your copies home and begin to sell or give them away.

* * *

In the novel *Fruit of the Lemon* by Andrea Levy, the main character, Faith, has been sent to Jamaica by her parents, who recognize that their daughter, born in England, is unsure of her identity as a black person in a mostly white society. Her idea growing up was that her family history began when her parents sailed from Jamaica in a banana boat and landed in England. After two weeks in Jamaica, among relatives who come in many ethnic varieties and in all shades of brown as well as white, Faith knows much about her heritage. Her family history began in previous centuries with people from different continents.

Her aunt tells her in leaving, "Well, now you know a little, Faith. But there is more. There is always more." Faith's says to herself: "They wrapped me in a family history and swaddled me tight in its stories. And I was taking that family to England. But it would not fit in a suitcase — I was smuggling it home."

When you write your story, your children and grandchildren will know where they came from. But there is always more, much more. Keep smuggling your family history to your children, grandchildren, and others any way you can. It provides the continuity and glue to hold the family together.

ADDITIONAL RESOURCES

To write well with depth about your family's story, or your own, read broadly and boldly in many areas. The following list is representative, not exhaustive. Look for experiences similar to your own, for specific information, and for inspiration about how other people wrote about their lives.

RECENT BOOKS ABOUT HER OWN
LIFE BY KATIE FUNK WIEBE

You Never Gave Me a Name: One Mennonite Women's Story. Cascadia Publishing, 2009. Autobiographical account of the author's lifelong search for an identity.

Border Crossing: A Spiritual Journey, revised edition. Cascadia Publishing, 2002. The story of Wiebe's inner journey while moving from a full-time career into her retirement years.

The Storekeeper's Daughter: A Memoir. Herald Press, 1997. The story of Wiebe's growing up in an immigrant family in northern Saskatchewan.

Alone: A Widow's Search for Joy. Tyndale House Publishers, 1976. Revised as *Alone: A Search for Joy*, Kindred Press, 1987. The story of Wiebe's widowhood. Out of print but sometimes available on the Internet.

Bless Me Too, My Father. Herald Press, 1988. The story of Wiebe's journey through the changes of her middle years. Out of print but sometimes available on the Internet.

Good Times with Old Times: How to Write Your Memoirs. Herald Press, 1979. Out of print but sometimes available on the Internet.

BOOKS ABOUT WRITING FAMILY AND PERSONAL HISTORIES

Daniel, Lois. *How to Write Your Own Life Story: The Classic Guide for the Nonprofessional Writer*, 4th edition. Chicago Review Press, 1997.

Fletcher, William. *Recording your Family History: A Guide to Preserving Oral History with Video Tape and Audio Tape*. Dodd, Mead & Company, 1986.

Zinsser, William. *Inventing the Truth: The Art and Craft of Memoir*, revised and expanded second edition. Houghton Mifflin, 1995.

A GENERAL BOOK ON WRITING

Zinsser, William. *On Writing Well: An informal guide to writing nonfiction*, 25th anniversary edition, Collins, 2001. This book should be on every writer's shelf.

BOOKS ABOUT LIFE STAGES

L'Engle, Madeleine. *The Irrational Season*. Seabury Press, 1977.

Sheehy Gail. *Passages. Predictable Crises of Adult Life*. E.P. Dutton, 1974.

Wiebe, Katie Funk, ed. *Life After Fifty: A Positive Look at Aging in the Faith Community*. Faith & Life Press, 1993.

Wiebe, Katie Funk. *Bridging the Generations*. Herald Press, 2001.

BOOKS ABOUT COLLECTING FOLKLORE

Beck, Ervin. *MennoFolk: Mennonite & Amish Folk Traditions*, Books 1 & 2. Herald Press, 2004 and 2005.

Brunvand, Jan Harold. *The Story of American Folklore: An Introduction*. W.W. Norton & Company, 1968. This is considered a classic in the area of folk tales and traditions.

Zeitlin, Steven J. et al. *A Celebration of American Family Folklore: Tales and Traditions from the Smithsonian Collection*. Pantheon Books, 1982.

BOOKS ABOUT FAITH AND LIFE JOURNEYS

Lee, Robert and Nancy V. Lee. *Making Sense of the Journey: The Geography of our Faith* (Mennonite stories integrating faith and life and the world of thought). Herald Press, 2007.

Wuthnow, Robert. *Growing Up Religious: Christians and Jews and Their Journeys of Faith*. Beacon Press, 1999.

HISTORICAL EVENTS

Egan, Timothy. *The Worst Hard Time: The Untold Story of Those Who Survived the Great American Dust Bowl*. Houghton Mifflin, 2006.

BIOGRAPHICAL AND AUTOBIOGRAPHICAL

Ayers, Esther Royer. *Rolling Down Black Stockings: A Passage Out of the Old Order Mennonite Religion*. Kent State University Press, 2005.

Angelou, Maya. *I Know Why the Caged Bird Sings*. Random House, 2009.

McCourt, Frank. *Angela's Ashes: A Memoir*. Scribner, 1996.

_____. *'Tis*. Scribner, 1999.

Walls, Jeanette. *The Glass Castle: A Memoir*. Scribner, 2005.

WRITING ABOUT ETHICAL WILLS

Baines, Barry K., M.D. *Ethical Wills: Putting Your Values on Paper*. Da Capo Press, 2006.

Johnson, Marilyn. *The Dead Beat: Lost Souls, Lucky Stiffs, and the Perverse Pleasures of Obituaries*. Harper Collins, 2006.

Turnbull, Susan B. *The Wealth of Your Life: A Step-by-Step Guide for Creating Your Ethical Will*. Benedict Press, 2005.

ABOUT THE AUTHOR

Katie Funk Wiebe, professor emeritus of Tabor College, Hillsboro, Kansas, retired in 1990 after teaching English for 24 years. She has devoted her retirement years to bringing meaning to life through writing and speaking.

Wiebe grew up in northern Saskatchewan, the daughter of Russian-German immigrants. With her husband and children she came to Kansas in 1962. Her husband died seven weeks later. That experience prompted the writing of her first book, *Alone: A Widow's Search for Joy*. She followed that with several other memoirs and personal histories. In addition to hundreds of articles, she has written and/or edited 18 books, focusing in the last years on aging.

The Mennonite Health Association honored her with the Anabaptist Healthcare Award for 1993 for her work in mental health, women's issues, and aging.

Wiebe is the mother of three children and grandmother of six. She lives in Wichita, Kansas.